CAMBRIDGE AIR SURVEYS

GENERAL EDITORS

DAVID KNOWLES   J. K. S. St JOSEPH

H. GODWIN

III

THE EARLY DEVELOPMENT OF IRISH SOCIETY

THE EARLY DEVELOPMENT OF IRISH SOCIETY

THE EVIDENCE OF AERIAL PHOTOGRAPHY

by

E. R. NORMAN

Lecturer in History in the
University of Cambridge

&

J. K. S. St JOSEPH

Director in Aerial Photography in the
University of Cambridge

WITH 70 AERIAL PHOTOGRAPHS

CAMBRIDGE

AT THE UNIVERSITY PRESS

1969

Published by the Syndics of the Cambridge University Press
Bentley House, 200 Euston Road, London N.W.1
American Branch: 32 East 57th Street, New York, N.Y.10022

© Cambridge University Press 1969

Library of Congress Catalogue Card Number: 71-85734
Standard Book Number: 521   07471   1

Printed in Great Britain
at the University Printing House, Cambridge
(Brooke Crutchley, University Printer)

CONTENTS

PREFACE

The aerial photographs upon which this book is based were obtained in flights forming part of the annual programmes of the Committee for Aerial Photography of the University of Cambridge. In each of the three years 1951, 1952 and 1955 a limited amount of photography was undertaken in Northern Ireland, but the bulk of the collection was obtained between 1963 and 1968. For a period of ten days each July the Committee's aircraft was based at Dublin, and reconnaissance flights were made over all parts of the country. Authority for the operations was kindly given by the Irish Department of Transport and Power. Negotiations with the official authorities concerned were greatly assisted by Dr A. T. Lucas, Director of the National Museum of Ireland; the resulting photographs owe much to his continued help during this period. The authors are grateful to Dr Kathleen Hughes, of Newnham College, who kindly gave advice before the manuscript went to press.

Till 1951 little aerial photography had been undertaken in Ireland specifically for research of this kind, indeed, much of the country was archaeologically unexplored. Thanks are due to those who initially furnished lists of suggestions for photography, particularly to Professor E. M. Jope in 1951, and to the staff of the National Museum and to Professor M. J. O'Kelly in connection with the more recent flights. As often happens with aerial photography, the very undertaking of the work posed new questions and suggested further subjects for study, for it is hardly possible to appreciate on the ground the extraordinarily wide range of historical and archaeological information preserved in the Irish landscape.

How to exploit this unexpected wealth of new knowledge, so rich in historical implication, presents its own special problems. Meanwhile, reconnaissance has already yielded some 10,000 photographs all illustrating one significant aspect or another of the Irish landscape. Further work would add to their number: many important sites remain undiscovered, or their significance not fully appreciated but the material already available, drawn from all parts of Ireland, is enough to be generally representative, and as a collection is unlikely easily to be superseded. Thus some publication of results so far seems due, even if it be but a preliminary account. The wide historical interest of the photographs caught the interest of Dr Edward Norman, whose work has lain mainly in the field of modern Irish history, and the present collaboration is the result. The choice of plates has been guided by the interest of the various sites and by the quality of the photographs. Many other places might have been illustrated, but the need to keep the book to a reasonable size has limited the choice to 70. It is hoped that later periods of Irish history may be the subject of a second volume.

J. K. ST JOSEPH

Cambridge, 30 May 1968

PHOTOGRAPHS

*The entry at the end of each caption gives the index letter and six-figure reference on the
National Grid, printed on the Ordnance Survey ½-inch to a mile maps*

ix

The air photographs are the copyright of the
University of Cambridge

ABBREVIATIONS

J.R.S.A.I.	Journal of the Royal Society of Antiquaries of Ireland
P.P.S.	Proceedings of the Prehistoric Society
P.R.I.A.	Proceedings of the Royal Irish Academy
T.R.I.A.	Transactions of the Royal Irish Academy
U.J.A.	Ulster Journal of Archaeology

The names of all other periodicals are given in full
in footnotes and bibliography

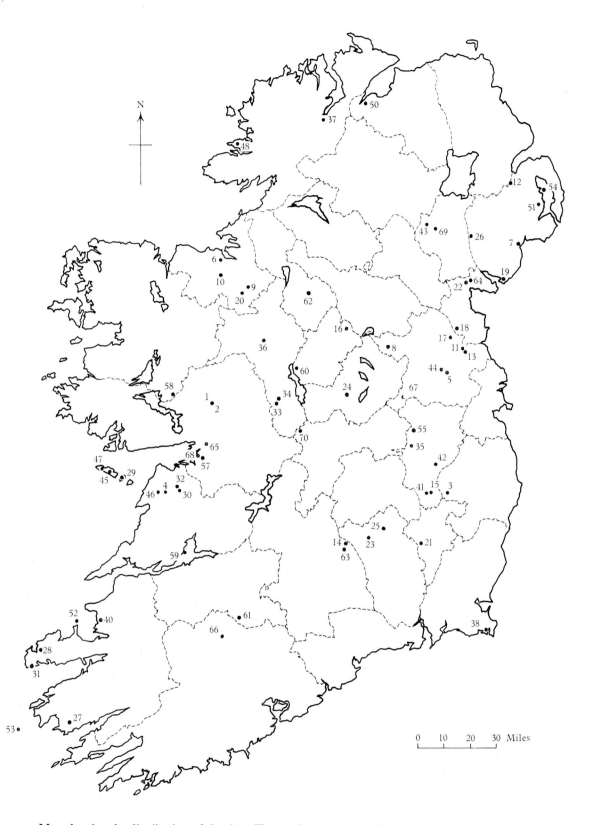

Map showing the distribution of the sites. The numbers correspond to the figure numbers in the text.

1

INTRODUCTION

DIFFERENT PARTS OF IRELAND have been photographed from the air to meet requirements of planning or to serve those concerned with the search for raw materials.[1] In such surveys the need is usually for vertical photographs, at a medium scale, and these may record, incidentally, many aspects of former land use. However, the development of archaeological air reconnaissance has shown that study from the air of ancient cultural landscapes is a subject with its own requirements which need to be fully understood if the best results are to be obtained.

In Ireland, pioneer work in this field goes back some forty years, to a decision of the Ancient Monuments Advisory Committee for Northern Ireland in 1927 which led to the photography of selected features by the Royal Air Force. The published results[2] include a 'mosaic' of the Dorsey entrenchments, vertical photographs of Navan and of a number of other important sites, besides photographs of features observed incidentally in the course of the work. By about 1934, the Irish Air Force also had recorded, in vertical or oblique views, a small number of well-known monuments.[3] The subjects illustrated in the reports of these two surveys are almost all earthworks, and the photographs demonstrate how careful attention has to be paid to lighting if the work is to yield the best results. Few buried sites were illustrated as if the conditions favouring their discovery, largely determined by the vagaries of Irish weather, were not then sufficiently understood. Further sites have been photographed from time to time, by Service aircraft or by commercial firms as opportunity offered: the results may be judged from the comparatively few photographs so far published.[4] However, given the right conditions there seemed no doubt whatever that Ireland offers great opportunities for this method of research, even if the work should prove to have an emphasis rather different from that in England. The recently issued first volume of an archaeological survey of Northern Ireland, describing the monuments in Co. Down, contains a generous selection of air photographs.[5]

[1] Cf., for example, the vertical photographs covering much of the Burren taken for the Ambassador Irish Oil Co., in 1962. The scale is about 1:20,000.
[2] D. A. Chart, *Antiquity*, IV (1930), 453–9, pls. i–vii.
[3] J. Raftery, *J.R.S.A.I.* LXXIV (1944), 119–23, pls. xi–xiii.
[4] J. Raftery, *Prehistoric Ireland* (1951), and S. P. Ó Ríordáin, *Antiquities of the Irish Countryside* (4th ed. 1964), include four and eight air photographs respectively.
[5] H.M.S.O., Belfast, 1966.

Air photographs display the present state of a landscape fashioned by nature and man. In western Europe, comparatively few areas of any size now remain untouched by human development. In countries long occupied by man, not only the existing pattern of settlement, but the whole cultural landscape, revealing successive stages of human settlement can, under favourable conditions, be discerned and recorded from the air. Features in relief, such as banks and ditches, mounds and hollows may be photographed by paying attention to shadows. The slighter the relief, as for example traces of ancient agriculture or very denuded earthworks, the more oblique the lighting needed to pick out significant detail. Conditions of very clear visibility are essential since atmospheric haze effectively diffuses sunlight when the sun is at a low altitude, so that images lack crispness. Photographs of this kind can be of the greatest value to field archaeologists in that they draw attention to features that may have escaped notice hitherto, often because of their remoteness from the beaten track. They can also bring fresh understanding to complicated earthworks, where the very extent of the visible remains means that complete comprehension of a site has eluded observers on the ground.

Changes in land use and the extension of agriculture inevitably mean that over large areas monuments and constructions of one age are destroyed or obliterated in another. When this happens, no visible features remain to guide the ground observer and past history is buried in levelled fields. It has, however, long been recognised that once the land has been disturbed by whatever agency, the soil and subsoil do not return to their natural compactness, and the effects of such disturbances remain practically for ever. Slight variations in colour and texture of the soil, best seen in bare fields after fresh ploughing, may provide a clue to structures long since obliterated. Even more important, vegetation growing over buried features continues to respond to hidden differences in the soil. This differential growth of vegetation, best seen in bird's-eye view, affords a clue to features long lost to sight. In well-established natural plant-communities, heath, moorland and rough pasture, it is geological variations that are mainly reflected in the vegetation, but, in agricultural land, growing crops respond in various ways to minor man-made disturbances. The effect depends much on the inter-relations of weather, soil and crops, but suffice to say that in Ireland, cereal crops growing on light soils have been observed to give the best results.

It will be appreciated that regional surveys designed to meet the needs of modern development cannot give the fullest archaeological information. Flights need to be planned in relation to the problems calling for solution. The weather, not only at the time of flying but during the whole active growth-period of the crops, the surface geology and the direction and intensity of lighting, have all to be considered. Much archaeological air survey is in the nature of reconnaissance undertaken to observe and photograph features not previously known to exist. To do this effectively calls for knowledge both of the distribution of the many categories of ancient sites and of the environments of early periods, so that regard may be paid to the effect of various factors that influenced a choice of site for settlement or fortification. Once identified, features can be recorded in oblique or vertical photographs (figs. 1 and 2). Oblique photographs from a low altitude are most readily understood by those unpractised in interpretation: in the present surveys they have been extensively used since in work of this kind they are the most economical of flying time. Vertical photographs are indispensable for an accurate rendering of plan, while for many aspects of scientific study, over-lapping vertical photographs are the most valuable of all.

The ways in which ancient sites may be identified from the air are varied, and many years' experience of such work has provided a sound basis for studying the inter-action of different conditions of soil, weather and crops. How wide was the scope for reconnaissance in Ireland was a question that often arose, since the pioneer work already mentioned was too limited to give much hint of what was to come. In Ireland, the relatively high rainfall; the Atlantic weather, even more variable than in England; the predominance of pasture; the small extent of arable land; and, for the most part, the absence of widespread new building, altering the historical pattern of towns and villages, were factors to take into account in gauging the results to be expected. The prospects appeared as a challenging opportunity not only to record man-made structures existing in the modern landscape, but also to reveal a whole succession of ancient cultural landscapes so essential to a full understanding of the settlement pattern of today. Moreover, the earlier the period of study the more important the setting of geology and vegetation, so that the wide scope of the enquiry will be apparent. Flights were planned to take account of suggestions put forward by official Departments and Institutions in Dublin and elsewhere, but the over-riding consideration was the need to record as many different aspects as possible of the past and present cultural landscape and of its natural background.

The highly specialised photographs that have been obtained in these brief surveys, though in no sense exhaustive, form a large enough collection to be broadly representative and to establish the lines on which future research should proceed. Reconnaissance has extended to every Irish county, the detailed progress of the work being determined by the incidence of weather favourable for photography: this inevitably restricted the time that could be spent over the mountain ranges.

Archaeological reconnaissance from the air commonly produces surprises, and these surveys are no exception. Perhaps the greatest surprise of all is the extent and variety of surviving earthworks. Of the productive agricultural land of Ireland, that is the surface excluding mountain and peat-bog, by far the greatest part is in pasture, seldom if ever ploughed in modern times. This has favoured the preservation of

3

Explanation to figures 1 and 2

The same earthworks are recorded in an oblique and a vertical photograph, both taken about 7.15 pm on 21 July 1967, in clear sunlight.

Near the centre of the oblique photograph (fig. 1) is a typical rath surrounded by remains of old field boundaries now seen as low earthen banks: a second rath lies in the distance. The earthworks stand out by reason of the shadows they cast, the effect being emphasised as the camera is facing into sun. Most of the area is also included within the vertical photograph (fig. 2), in which the earthworks are picked out by scattered light reflected from their crests: these appear lighter in tone than the ground elsewhere.

Comparison of the two photographs emphasises the effect of obliquity in introducing a variable scale, so that in fig. 1, the shape of the earthworks appears distorted.

4

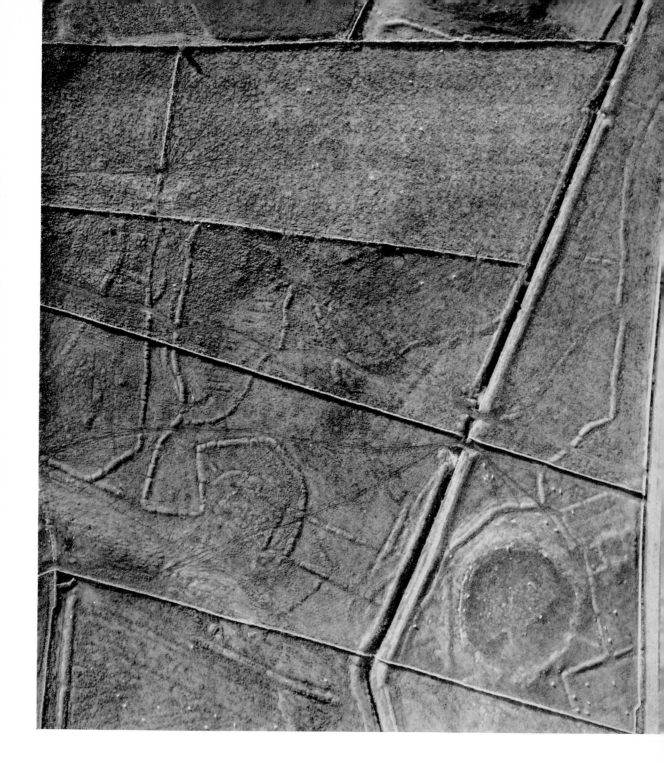

earthworks. Nowhere else in western Europe are the corrugations of the surface representing activities of ancient man so clearly visible over large areas.

For the earliest archaeological periods no man-made structures have survived that are now recognisable from the air. Thus air photographs can only demonstrate some of the factors governing a choice of site, a matter of great importance in a search for further traces of early settlement. A belt of sand dunes on a lee-shore would provide shelter; the relatively dry ground afforded by an ancient strand-line, less encumbered by vegetation than the wet soils elsewhere, was particularly inviting. Such geographical features can readily be illustrated and, indeed, have often survived but little changed.

The comprehensive nature of the aerial view means that the whole extent of a complicated site like a great Megalithic cemetery can be illustrated far more effectively in an aerial photograph (fig. 8) than in any view taken on the ground. Such photographs are also of value for demonstrating the relationship or juxtaposition of structures of different character. The photographs of Knocknashee and of the Bricklieve Mountains, in Co. Sligo (figs. 10 and 9) raise the important question whether the small circular features there visible are contemporary habitations. The value of this quality of comprehension appears again and again in the photographs. Thus, the numerous earthworks at Tara (fig. 44), can be seen in a single view impossible to obtain from any one point on the surface. A reader looking through the plates will also appreciate the value of oblique photographs taken from a low altitude for illustrating a site in relation to its surroundings.

That cropmarks would appear was only to be expected; that they should be so widespread and of such variety was unforeseen. Altogether upwards of five hundred different features have been identified in terms of cropmarks: most lie in the east and south-east of the country reflecting the greater extent of arable land there. The commonest situations in which they occur are on the crests of drumlins, on hummocks of glacial gravel and sand, or on gravels of river terraces, all places with a porous subsoil where a fall in the water-table in summer favours differential growth in cereal crops distinguishing where the ground had been anciently disturbed.

Round barrows are well known though not widespread in Ireland. Continued ploughing may easily destroy the mound of a barrow, especially one of no great size, but a surrounding ditch, filled with silted earth or plough-soil promotes, under suitable conditions, a growth of vegetation different from normal. These 'ring-ditches', long recognised on the chalk lands and in the river valleys of England, have appeared in various parts of Ireland. More than fifty destroyed barrows have been recorded in this way. Usually there is a single ditch, though examples with two or three ditches have also been seen. Near Lisduff Bridge (Tipperary) a group of some ten small circular ditches beside a 'ring-ditch' of normal size recalls the 'ring-ditch clusters' recently identified in England. No doubt chambered-cairns, heavily damaged by ploughing, await discovery. Once the principal stones have been removed the most likely clue, in the absence of a ditch, would probably be a patch of discoloured soil best seen after fresh ploughing. None have been noted in recent surveys, but these surveys have taken place in summer, while the optimum time for observation of such soil marks is the late autumn or early spring.

The great hill-forts, like their counterparts in Britain, lend themselves particularly

3   Hill-fort, Rathcoran, Baltinglass Hill, Co. Wicklow

well to photography from the air. Photographs can demonstrate both the choice of site and structural details of the earthworks, so helping to answer questions as to the way in which these huge enclosures were built. The view of Rathcoran, on Baltinglass Hill (fig. 3), demonstrates the widely spaced ramparts and the irregular excavations between them: the hollows serve to break up this belt of ground as an additional defence,[1] and no doubt yielded material for the construction of the ramparts.

On an unnamed hill, 977 feet high, some four miles north-east of Castledermot, Co. Kildare, a new example has been recorded.[2] The widely spaced ditches appeared as soil marks: the ramparts, formerly enclosing some 15 acres, are almost levelled, but the scatter of rubble that composed them can still be seen when the land is ploughed. The earthworks on Muckelty Hill, $2\frac{1}{2}$ miles north-east of Tobercurry,

[1] For the cairn see P. J. Walshe, *P.R.I.A.* XLVI C (1942), 221. There is a somewhat similar arrangement on the west side of the hill-fort at Old Oswestry, Salop.

[2] The earthwork at the summit, marked on the 1909 ed. of the O.S. 6-inch sheet Kildare 38, is a boundary of a former plantation.

Co. Sligo, seem to be remains of a small hill-fort unrecognised before,[1] and scrutiny of other isolated hill-tops will no doubt reveal more. This is an important field of study, since excavation of these structures offers a promising means of research into the social and economic conditions of the period.

The existence in Ireland of tens of thousands of raths is well known. Even when allowance is made for the fact that rath-building continued for centuries, this is the earliest visible archaeological expression of an expansion of population that led to the spread of farming settlements over the whole country. They are for the most part delineated on the first edition of the large scale maps of the Ordnance Survey,[2] for these were early enough to record many earthworks reduced or levelled by agriculture in the last hundred years. Less familiar are the ancient field-systems extensively preserved, for example, on the limestone outcrops in Clare, Galway and Roscommon, but appearing in many other places. The photograph of small fields near Kilfenora, in Co. Clare (fig. 4) gives some idea of the extent of such earthworks and the scope for interpretation. An access-way with parallel walls, meanders between the fields, and the position of farmsteads having enclosures of stone (cashels) may be distinguished, all over-ridden by the straight boundaries of modern fields. Since the photograph was taken, part of the site has been cleared for agriculture. The bare limestone in the left foreground of the plate shows the extent to which soil has wasted away since the ancient fields were laid out. The very number of cashels in parts of the Burren suggests that the country must formerly have been capable of supporting a greater population than now. The defensive character of some of these settlements is emphasised by the extraordinary *cheveaux de frise* round a neighbouring cashel at Ballykinvarga (fig. 46).

The Irish climate favours the use of the land for pasture, while over large districts the subdivision into small fields has so far acted as a disincentive to the introduction of deep tractor-drawn ploughs, a technique hardly economic unless applied to large units of land. In agricultural land raths may remain as uncultivated islands, surviving as rough grazing, or their banks may be incorporated in modern field-boundaries. The interior, if not ploughed today, very often carries the narrow strips of rundale cultivation so that buildings or structures contemporary with the rath are seldom visible and are invariably too slight to have been marked on the large scale maps of the first Ordnance Survey. However, the existence of these structures can be demonstrated in air photographs taken in very oblique lighting which picks out slight undulations of the surface. They appear as square or circular huts, either free-standing or attached to the bank enclosing the rath (fig. 34).

[1] The hill-fort is not marked on the first ed. (1837) of the O.S. 6-inch sheet Sligo 32. On the 1914 ed. an earthwork is shown in generalised outline.

[2] O.S. maps of Ireland, 6-inch scale, 1834–44. Earthworks are usually rendered in far better detail on the first edition of these maps than on later editions.

4 Cashels and associated fields, Kiltennan South, ENE. of Kilfenora, Co. Clare

Where earthworks are well preserved, so that raths can be seen in relation to other monuments, the air photograph may be able to demonstrate an order of succession. Perhaps the most important instances are provided by the occurrence, in relation to a rath, of irregular mounds and banks of the kind sometimes suggestive of later settlement (fig. 23). Here, careful study of photographs taken under the right conditions is an essential prerequisite to the excavation of such a site.

As might be expected, the greatest number of cropmarks are of raths, levelled by modern ploughing: in all some hundred and sixty examples, previously unknown, have come to light. The importance of these discoveries lies not in their numbers, but in the structural details only visible as cropmarks. Differences in the growth of crop, and less often in the colour of the soil, reveal not only the bank and the ditch, or ditches, surrounding these enclosed farmsteads, but also smaller features as well. Within the enclosure, the position of buildings or structures may be discerned, while clustered round the rath, the outlines of small pens or fields occasionally appear as thin spidery lines in the growing crop. Excavation alone can determine whether the small ditches revealed by these cropmarks were supplemented by stakes or thorn bushes to form an effective boundary.

The photographs also provide evidence for a number of rath-like enclosures grouped together (figs. 40 and 41). Whenever land immediately surrounding a rath is under cereal crops the area will be well worth scrutiny from the air. It may chance that only one member of a group has survived, and now that the existence of fields in relation to raths has been demonstrated (fig. 35), further instances of such associations will surely come to light. Occasionally cropmarks reveal conjoined raths, or raths with a substantial enclosure—perhaps a cattle-pound—attached to them, while replanning of the site may introduce further complications. Local and regional variations are to be anticipated: many thousands of raths have an enclosing bank of earth and stones, but this feature may not have been invariable. Near Bannow, Co. Wexford, where the ground is now subdivided into a number of small fields under various crops, part of the circuit of an enclosure has been seen. There are cropmarks, not only of ditches, but also of a very narrow disturbance like the palisade trenches well known at certain Iron Age sites in Scotland. A similar arrangement has been recorded at Duncormick, Co. Wexford, and at Grangerosnolvan, four miles east-south-east of Athy, in Kildare, and it would be no surprise to find that many more

GRANGEROSNOLVAN UPPER   NEWTOWN   DUNCORMICK

100 0   800 FEET   100   0   200 METRES

Sketch-plan of three farming settlements plotted from cropmarks. In each, the narrow line defining the inner circuit probably represents a palisade trench. Grangerosnolvan Upper—S 748908: Newtown—S 840097: Duncormick—S 925094.

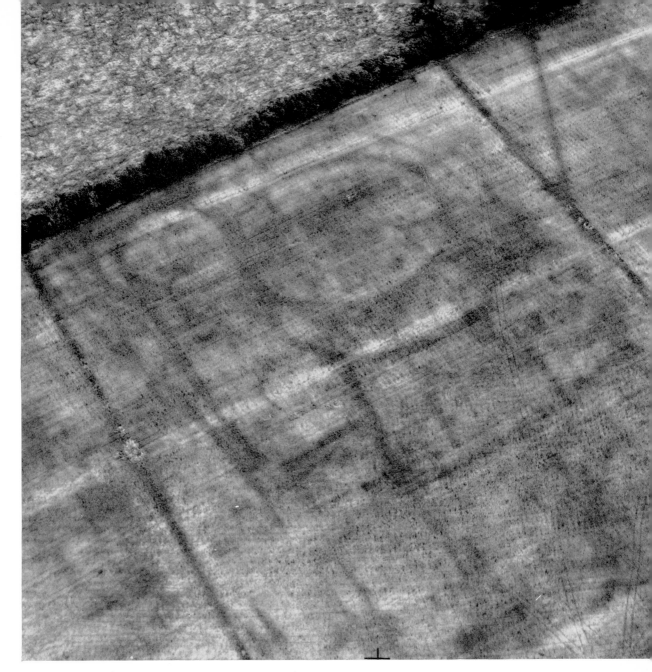

5 Complicated cropmarks, half a mile south-east of Tara, Co. Meath

await discovery.[1] The absence of a substantial enclosure-bank would make such sites all the more liable to destruction by modern agriculture.

Other features recorded as cropmarks deserve brief mention. There are a few instances of settlement sites of some complexity: whether they begun as raths, or whether rath-like enclosures were incorporated in them is not clear on present evidence. They are the nearest approach yet seen in Ireland to the complex 'settlements' of the Upper Thames valley. One such farmstead, comprising a rath re-planned more than once, lies only half a mile south-east of Tara (fig. 5) and this

[1] The cropmarks in question are so faint that they could not be reproduced effectively on a half-tone plate.

raises the important question whether the surroundings of such royal residences may not have been dotted with the substantial farmsteads necessary to support the population concentrated there. Most of the land around Tara is today in pasture, and it would be worth keeping careful watch on any fields under corn to see if further sites of this kind can be identified.

The cropmarks by the west shore of Lady's Island Lake, in south Wexford (fig. 38) seem quite new in Irish archaeology. The pattern of small rectangular field-plots recorded on the photograph resembles the so-called 'Celtic fields' of Wessex, while the similar fields of the Roman Iron Age in Denmark provide an even closer comparison, so far as the size of the plots is concerned. This can hardly be the sole remains of such agriculture in Ireland. Further surveys should be directed to determining the extent of the system, and its relation to other monuments. Another feature unrecognised before in Ireland was noticed in the Slaney valley near Enniscorthy. A line of small dots, each marking the position of a hole or pit, a few feet across, recalls the features commonly called 'pit-alignments' known over wide areas of the river valleys of eastern England, and proved to be of late Iron Age or Roman date.[1] In England they have to do with the partitioning or subdivision of land, and it will be interesting to see where further examples come to light. The absence of cropmarks of medieval sites may be noticed. In point of date some raths extend well into the Christian period, but deserted settlements, early monastic sites, and ruined churches almost invariably lie under pasture never yet disturbed by modern ploughing. Only at Drumacoo, Co. Galway, do extensive traces of buildings and accessways of an early monastic site appear as differences in tone of soil or vegetation (fig. 68).

Study of the early Celtic Christian church did not seem a promising field for research by air photography, yet reconnaissance of a representative number of these early sites has yielded abundant new knowledge of their physical remains beyond hope or expectation. At some of the most famous centres, like Clonmacnois and Glendalough, the ground surface is now so changed by spreading graveyards, or otherwise altered by modern use of the land, that air photography is not profitable. However, in contrast to the scant information so far obtained by air photography of Celtic Christian centres in Wales and Scotland, at many Irish sites earthworks survive in unexpected degree.

Air photographs of Skellig Michael and Illauntannig, showing a few beehive clochán clustered beside a tiny church with its burial-ground, display the character of these early Celtic Christian sites and demonstrate the extremes of solitude sought by men who practised the new Faith. Other sites were less remote; however, a distant valley, an island within a lake, an isolated hill-top, firm ground surrounded

---

[1] See *A Matter of Time, an archaeological survey*, R.C.H.M., England (1960), pp. 28–31.

by bog, are typical situations of these Celtic houses. In these places, an ancient graveyard, the grass-grown ruins of a primitive church and of other buildings, may be all that is now visible, though later structures, namely churches and perhaps a round tower, may have been added if the earliest site continued in being as a Christian centre. More often than not grassy mounds now mark the sites that were soon disused, for there were no substantial structures to survive, and both the weather and wandering animals must have toppled masonry and dislodged gravestones so that a cemetery may appear as no more than a hummocky area slightly mounded above the surrounding land. The remains are easily mistaken for a church or cill of much later date, or even for a deserted medieval settlement.

The extent of the earthworks at these early monastic centres is one of the surprises of recent work. At Clonard (see chapter 5), amongst the most famous sites of all, at Holy Island in Lough Derg,[1] at Inchcleraun,[2] and at Devenish,[3] there are extensive earthworks that have never received the attention they deserve, while at Fenagh, Shrule, Kiltiernan, and Ardpatrick, to mention a few sites, air photographs reveal large enclosures some two or three hundred feet in diameter much subdivided by small banks. In some of these compounds traces of buildings appear. At other places, such as Tarramud, Co. Galway and Rathcline, Co. Longford, the course of an enclosing wall can be recognised in whole or in part, but no internal structures remain visible. Clonmacnois and Glendalough cannot now be excavated because of the continued use of the land for burial, but these other centres offer the archaeologist remarkable opportunities, occurring nowhere else on a comparable scale, for the study of the early Celtic church.

Experience of the last five years permits an appreciation of the possibilities open to future reconnaissance. The greatest scope is no doubt for the photography of earthworks. It is seldom realised how limited are the periods of weather favourable for aerial photography. The need to choose, for such operations, a time of year most likely to offer sustained good weather has meant that hitherto reconnaissance has been confined to the summer. However, conditions of clear sunlight and good visibility may be seized at any time of year. The greatest chance for seeing soil marks will be after the peak periods of ploughing in autumn and spring. The differences in colour of the soil are often clearest when the surface of the ground is drying rapidly after heavy rainfall. A light covering of snow gives an even-toned background very suitable for the photography of earthworks, with the advantage that the white surface increases the effective brightness of sunlight otherwise too weak for photography in winter months save at midday. No observations of large peat-bogs under snow have

[1] R. A. S. Macalister, *P.R.I.A.* XXXIIIC (1917), 93–174 and especially the sketch-plan, pl. vii.
[2] F. J. Bigger, *J.R.S.A.I.* XXX (1901), 69–90, but with no plan of the earthworks.
[3] *Preliminary Survey of the Ancient Monuments of Northern Ireland* (H.M.S.O., Belfast, 1940), p. 161.

6 Panorama of hilly country north of Coolaney, Co. Sligo, looking east

been attempted: it would be interesting, indeed, if the fleeting effects produced by differential melting might reveal the position of crannógs or track-ways submerged in such bogs. Many of the effects mentioned are transient and there is always the practical difficulty of organising reconnaissance at short notice.

The photographs are also of value for an understanding of the natural background of these ancient sites. When looking at the illustrations in this book the reader is invited to think away the modern landscape, often with a trim pattern of enclosed fields, to try to recapture a very different world untamed by man. In all Ireland, the large peat-bogs and the surface of the higher mountains alone may have appeared to the Megalithic peoples as they appear to us today, though climatic changes and the grazing of animals may even there have caused significant differences in vegetation. The hilly country in Co. Sligo, illustrated in fig. 6, has always been free of agricultural encroachments, and its tangled slopes may have seemed much the same in prehistoric times as now. Elsewhere the surface detail of modern Ireland is largely the work of man. From the summit of one of the isolated hills that rise above the surrounding central plain it is still possible to gather some impression of the natural wilderness of moor and bog, fen and forest, in which these hills were formerly set. In detail, the changes that have taken place are great indeed. The felling of forests, the clearance of land, the draining of bogs, the cutting of peat, the dredging of rivers, have brought in their train a lowering of the water-table and changes in vegetation that have produced a very different landscape. It is the business of Quaternary research in conjunction with archaeology to study and record these changes, and the task is urgent since 'development' of all kinds is today taking place at a greater rate than ever before, as mechanical aids are brought in to assist modern exploitation of the land. Thus these air surveys display the Irish landscape in transition. Vast peat-bogs still remain, but a view from the air of the progress of mechanised peat cutting necessary to feed a modern power-station, or of the grouping together of small fields in the rationalisation of agriculture for mechanised farming, leaves no doubt that the present landscape will not long survive. Planning can take account of visible remains, but no degree of planning can allow for hidden features of which not a trace appears on the surface. Aerial survey is the only way of discovering such buried sites, and it is the only practicable way of recording the innumerable earthworks found in all parts of the country. There is thus need for a carefully planned programme of photography before new building, quarrying, afforestation, and more intensive agriculture change the face of the land for ever.

2

BEFORE THE CELTS

THERE SEEM TO HAVE BEEN no movements of Paleolithic peoples following the wild deer into Ireland during the closing sequences of the Ice Age. The country was then, with Britain, still joined to the European land mass. By around 6,000 B.C. the protracted adjustments in relative level of land and sea following the retreat of the Quaternary glaciers led to subsidence which ended this state of affairs, and inroads of the sea severed Ireland from Britain. Warm and relatively dry climatic conditions prevailed, favouring the growth of sub-Boreal forests; but there remained, as places suitable for human habitation, the modest summits of the drumlins which extended across the northern half of the country. The sandy ridges of glacial gravel known as eskers, the sandhills by rivers and sea-shores, a few open grasslands and the higher slopes of hills also provided possible sites for settlement. The first inhabitants of Ireland—the Mesolithic food-gathering peoples—settled in some of these open places. First they came to the extreme north-east, perhaps attracted by the chalk and flint outcrops which exist only there: more, indeed, than exist now, for the continuing advance of the sea submerged many of their first settlements. Of these earliest people little is known. Probably their ultimate origin lay somewhere in Scandinavia, or around the fringes of the North Sea. The details of their movements cannot now be determined. No settlement sites are known in Ireland, but probably they were nomadic: their temporary camps may have resembled the excavated site at Starr Carr in Yorkshire. They lived by hunting and fishing. In Ireland a few of their rubbish-pits, and quite a lot of their skilfully-worked flint tools, are their only tangible memorial.

The Mesolithic food-gatherers retreated from the arrival of new groups of immigrants who brought early Neolithic culture to Ireland. They moved from the north-eastern coastal areas up the River Bann, and then beyond to seek refuge in other river valleys. The newcomers took over the coastal sites which they had vacated and then also began to penetrate the interior of the country. Some of the earliest Neolithic remains have been identified in the Dundrum sandhills in Co. Down (fig. 7). The dating of finds from these sites is very difficult, especially as cultural periods overlapped on such an extensive scale. But it is clear that the dunes contain the débris of settlement from early Neolithic to early medieval times. The chief sandspit in the Murlough peninsula at Dundrum is typical of early coastal sites in the north of Ireland. The dunes consist of sand blown originally onto a raised beach;

16

7   Prehistoric settlement site, Dundrum Sandhills, Co. Down

the highest hillocks rising to over a hundred feet. The early remains are found in stratified bands running through the dunes: these are stains produced by charcoal, decayed vegetable matter, and the general refuse of habitation lying on the surface before movements of the sand buried them. But finds of various ages are intermixed, and the lowest bands at one place in the dunes are not necessarily contemporary with the lowest at another.[1] Flints, potsherds, and middens of shells and bones of the Neolithic periods are to be found here—alongside Bronze Age metal slag and burial cists. A small group of post-holes, discovered during excavations in 1951, was associated with Neolithic finds, and there can be little doubt that this was the site of a wooden hut of the period. Constant shifting of the sand makes dating unreliable.

The Neolithic settlement of Ireland established communities with outside links and a reasonably uniform culture. That agriculture became known—itself an indication of the extent of these external connections—is proved by the occasional survival of querns. Trade was sometimes over long distances: the products of the late Neo-

[1] A. E. P. Collins, 'Excavations in the Sandhills at Dundrum, 1950–1', in *U.J.A.* xv (1952), 25.

lithic axe-factory at Tievebulliagh in Co. Antrim have been located in north-east Scotland and the Thames Valley as well as scattered in parts of Ireland itself. The axe trade was based upon a seam of porcellanite rock exposed on the eastern face of Tievebulliagh mountain. This site, and another one on Rathlin Island, were the only known places with porcellanite outcrops at the surface. Below the summit at Tievebulliagh are scree-like mounds of waste from the early workings, and it is here that many of the flakes, chips, and partly worked 'rough-outs' of the axe industry have been found. The existence of the factory and its products 'opens up vistas of extensive trading in late Neolithic times throughout the British Isles which are sometimes hardly even hinted at by evidence from other sources'.[1] Certainly the mobility of their trading suggests skills in boat-building and navigation hitherto unsuspected.

While the Tievebulliagh factory was at the height of its productivity, new groups of settlers began to enter the country. They came from the eastern Mediterranean early in the third millenium B.C., settling first in the Iberian peninsula and then reaching Ireland (around 3,000 B.C. or earlier) both directly, by sea, and from Brittany where some of them had established colonies. They also extended further to the north, settling in Denmark and northern Germany. The impressive odyssey of these people was spread over more than a thousand years. They practised agriculture—and metal craft. Their search for fresh sources of copper may, indeed, have been the initial impulse which directed them towards the western seas. There are also signs that two distinct cultural groups may have been involved: one building passage-graves for their dead, the other gallery-graves.[2] For these newcomers to Ireland were the Megalithic peoples, the builders of those immense stone sepulchres which even today testify their remarkable skills and social organization. It is, in fact, from their tombs that almost all knowledge of them must derive, for of their actual settlements there are scant remains. Upon light soils at Lough Gur, Co. Limerick, Professor Ó Ríordáin excavated some houses of the period, though whether these belonged to the actual Megalithic peoples, or to Irish Neolithic natives under their influence is not clear.[3] These houses were wood-framed with rush-thatched roofs, both round and rectangular in shape. From the remains it is clear that they grew crops and kept cows, pigs and sheep. They also used flint tools imported from Tievebulliagh. No examples of their metal craft have yet been found either at the Lough Gur settlement or in any of their tombs. Perhaps the Megalithic peoples did not find the sources of copper they had hoped to—the Neolithic farmers among whom they

---

[1] E. M. Jope, 'Porcellanite Axes from Factories in North-east Ireland: Tievebulliagh and Rathlin', in *U.J.A.* xv (1952), 32.

[2] G. E. Daniel, 'The Dual Nature of the Megalithic Colonization of Prehistoric Europe', in *P.P.S.* VII (1941), 41.

[3] See S. P. Ó Ríordáin, 'Lough Gur Excavations', in *J.R.S.A.I.* LXXVII (1947), 81, and 'Prehistory in Ireland' in *P.P.S.* XIII (1947), 147.

settled in Ireland could not have helped them in this, since metal was not known to them—or perhaps they discovered it and mined it, and exported it to the parent colonies in Iberia, as Dr Daniel has suggested.[1]

The term 'Megalithic' is applied to all those peoples whose tombs were built of slabs of stone, or by cutting into rock surfaces. There was a general cultural unity about the European Megalithic peoples, but diversities expressed themselves in various architectural styles and these can be classified. The obvious main distinction lies between passage-graves and gallery-graves. The latter are subdivided into court cairns and wedge-shaped graves. Ó Ríordáin and Daniel additionally distinguished between entrance-graves and portal-dolmens.[2] De Valera has been content to divide the monuments into four main classes.[3] But whatever refinements are adopted it remains clear that, in Irish terms, the broad cultural unity of the Megalithic peoples was in practice expressed in some four of five variations. Furthermore, classifications of the people who built the tombs according to different types of architectural style is sustained by a classification based upon the grave-goods discovered in them: an indication of the general reliability of architectural classification as a broad guide to cultural variations. The actual date of Irish Megalithic tombs must be considered, of course, in relation to individual examples, but it is reasonably certain that chambered tombs were being constructed in Brittany as early as 3,500 B.C., and were used and built as late as 1,000 B.C. The Brittany comparison is an especially useful one since one of the most striking cultural characteristics of the passage-graves of eastern Ireland is their sophisticated art. Similar designs—spirals, zig-zags, chevrons—are found upon the stones of the Brittany monuments. There are, in Ireland, about 4,000 remaining Megalithic chambered tombs, and many may still rest undetected in the countryside. Still more of the accessible and less-substantially built tombs must have been destroyed. The different types are usually associated with regional concentrations, and this also suggests local cultural variations among the groups of colonising peoples. For these variations may well have already existed when the settlers arrived in Ireland, since there is no evidence to indicate that one style is necessarily a degeneration of another. It is unlikely, for example, that the Carrowmore passage-graves of Co. Sligo, which lack the corballed roof technique and elaborate entrance-ways of some of the Boyne monuments, are, as was once believed,[4] a decadent version of eastern proto-types. Probably local building materials dictated the differences, and the ready accessibility of large blocks to serve as capstones made corballing simply unnecessary.

[1] S. P. Ó Ríordáin and Glyn Daniel, *Newgrange* (London, 1964), p. 139.
[2] *Ibid.* p. 144.
[3] R. de Velera and S. Ó Nualláin, *Survey of the Megalithic Tombs of Ireland*, vol. I, *Clare* (Dublin, 1961), p. xii.
[4] T. G. E. Powell, 'The Passage Graves of Ireland', in *P.P.S.* IV (1938), 243.

It has to be admitted that when it comes to sites like the Megalithic tombs, the techniques of aerial photography have only limited application. A view from the sky most usefully shows a particular monument in relation to natural features, highlighting the choice of site by the builders. But this may be all that it can demonstrate. These tombs were originally covered with heaps of small stones, and where they have survived an aerial photograph will simply show a grass-covered mound or a mountain-top cairn. Where the covering materials have been removed, the orthostats and capstones of the internal chamber may remain, but aerial photographs will reveal nothing that is not obvious on the ground. Occasionally sites associated with the tombs are revealed as cropmarks—and it is in such fortuitous occurrences that most discoveries are to be looked for in the future.

Of all the Megalithic types, it is the passage-graves which most impressively suggest the high skills and technical accomplishments of these early peoples. Passage-graves were generally built upon hill-tops or, if there were no actual hills, as at the Bend of the Boyne, on the highest available ground, and they were commonly grouped in cemeteries. Similar methods of construction were probably adopted everywhere. A series of large kerb-stones were laid down to describe a circle, and large orthostats were built inwards towards the centre from an opening on one side. This passage led to a chamber, characteristically of cruciform shape, with a corballed or capstone ceiling higher than that of the entrance tunnel. While the chamber was being built small stones were piled up within the kerb-stones forming a mound which covered the actual tomb. As a finish, the side of the cairn nearest to the entrance was sometimes faced with white quartzite pebbles. Building materials were not—like the 'bluestones' of Stonehenge—brought from very great distances. All the stones used at Newgrange, for example, could have been gathered from within a ten mile radius of the monument itself. For the large orthostats, however, there must still have been formidable problems of transportation.

Passage-graves were for communal burials, and usually for cremated remains, though examples of inhumation are known. The scale of the larger tombs must surely indicate the superior status of the deceased: they must have been for chieftains and their families. Less distinguished tombs are frequently grouped around the great mounds, and these indicate less august occupants. There were also many simple cist burials for the least important persons. An hierarchical social order is thus faithfully reflected in these burial arrangements. But the passage-graves are not necessarily pointers to the locations of Megalithic settlement. Many of the hill sites chosen must have enjoyed ritual significance, but it is not as yet possible to determine whether the populations who built the tombs actually lived in the immediate neighbourhood. No domestic settlements associated with a passage-grave cemetery have yet been found in the eastern part of Ireland, and the hypothesis that 'hut' sites on two mountains in Co. Sligo may be the dwellings of the people who built the great nearby cairns is only tentative, however strongly the evidence would seem to point in that direction.

There are between 150 and 200 known passage-graves in Ireland. Probably the original number was never very much greater than this, since the huge size of most of the cairns, and their situation on hill-tops, cannot have invited the vandalism of farmers and road-builders who robbed the stones of so many gallery-graves on lower ground. A few passage-graves are apparently isolated, like the 'Mound of the Hostages' at Tara. But most are grouped together in cemeteries: at the Bend of the Boyne, at Loughcrew in Co. Meath, at Carrowmore and Carrowkeel in Co. Sligo. Some of the isolated graves can be arranged within a geographical unity, like the 'Dublin Group' of six monuments on the tops of the northern fringe of the Wicklow Mountains. At Loughcrew the passage-grave cemetery is fairly concentrated within a small upland area (fig. 8). This must at one time have comprised a group of above thirty separate mounds, but many have been destroyed and only the larger examples remain. These range from 50 to 200 feet in diameter. The cruciform pattern of the internal chamber can be clearly seen where it has been exposed by the excavation of one of the smaller cairns. This is 'Cairn H', 55 feet in diameter, about the date of which there has been so much controversy—but it is almost certainly, like the group as a whole, to be dated to between 3,000 and 2,000 B.C.[1] Some of the stones at Loughcrew are decorated, like those of the Boyne tombs. At Carrowmore, in Co. Sligo, an even greater proportion of the original number of chambered cairns has been destroyed. Here the cemetery extends over an area a mile long and half a mile wide, and it is situated not upon hills, but upon a fairly level plain. There were once rather more than sixty tombs,[2] but gravel-quarrying has bitten into the group and only thirty-two remain. The surviving monuments—as has already been noticed— lack many of the more impressive technical and artistic characteristics of eastern passage-graves: there are no corballed roofs, entrance-passages are extremely short, and none of the orthostats or kerb-stones are decorated. But three are cruciform in design, and most have retained some portion of their covering cairns. All are small, with average diameters of forty feet or so. It has sometimes been suggested that the Carrowmore group represents an independent colony of Megalithic peoples who entered the country directly from Iberia *via* the western sea route.[3]

County Sligo is also rich in mountain-top cairns, and at Carrowkeel in the Brick- lieve Mountains, a group of thirteen cairns built upon the highest points of five lime- stone ridges contain passage-graves. Two other mounds cover Megalithic cist burials. All these monuments were constructed when the mountains—which attain over a

---

[1] Ó Ríordáin and Daniel, *Newgrange*, pp. 100–1, and 122–4.
[2] W. C. Borlase, *The Dolmens of Ireland* (London, 1897), vol. I, p. 142.
[3] Estyn Evans, *Prehistoric and Early Christian Ireland* (London, 1966), p. 188.

8 Passage-grave cemetery, Loughcrew, Co. Meath

thousand feet—were bare of vegetation. At some later time several feet of peat
accumulated, and the existing heather which covers the ridges rests on top of it.[1] One
known cairn, and perhaps some others, were completely buried by the rise of the
peat. In 1911 all the tombs were investigated by Macalister and others, but not with

[1] R. A. S. Macalister, E. C. R. Armstrong and R. Ll. Praeger, 'Report on the Excavation of Bronze-Age
Cairns on Carrowkeel Mountain', in *P.R.I.A.* XXIX C (1912), 314.

too felicitous a result. For their methods were, by modern practice, unscientific, and the opportunity to add a considerable amount to knowledge about these types of monuments and the people who built them was largely missed. For unlike the other known passage-graves, the Carrowkeel tombs were still intact when opened. Their cairns were found to have been built of loose stones, piled within kerbs, and still surviving to heights of over twenty feet. Most of the chambers were cruciform, and many had corbalied roofs. Both inhumation and cremation had been practiced, though the latter was by far the more common burial custom.[1] 'Carrowkeel' pottery was found, and bone pins and beads; but no metal objects. All the tombs appear to belong to the same cultural period.

As important as the passage-grave cemetery at Carrowkeel, however, is the large group of 'hut' sites clustered on the flattened ridge below the so-called Carn 'O' (which contains a Megalithic cist). On this fissured rock surface, 800 feet high, between the base of the summit cliff and a townland wall, are an amazing number of small circular enclosures—Macalister drew forty-seven on his plan of this 'village',[2] but twice that number are visible from the air (fig. 9). The construction of the 'huts' is rough but not haphazard. They have two rings of upright stone slabs with small stones between them, to give a wall some three feet in thickness. They range between 20 and 42 feet in diameter. Since only the foundations remain it is impossible to speculate about the original appearance of these structures. None appear to have doorways, and most are clearly too large to have had corbalied roofs. Thatch is unthinkable at this altitude and in so exposed a position, though wood, from the abundant forests which once crept up to the foot of the mountain, could have provided roofing materials. The structures were probably not actual dwellings, how-ever, but wind-shields and protective enclosures against wild animals within which wooden huts were built. Were these stone enclosures the homes of the Megalithic peoples who built the cairns for their dead? That cannot be assured. But it is difficult to see where else these people could have lived. The surrounding land was then forest-covered, and even the inhospitable and bare mountain ridges, rising out of the forests, must have seemed preferable to the damp and wolf-infested lowlands. Unfortunately the 'village' site is so exposed upon the naked rock that no profitable excavation is possible there. If these small enclosures were the homes of the cairn-builders, then they have left nothing behind to show it.

Two miles to the north-west of Carrowkeel is Keshcorran, with its particularly striking cairn high upon the 1,188 foot summit. It is the setting of many legendary happenings, and a place, even today, of annual celebration.[3] The cairn has not yet been excavated. There are caves half-way up the western face of the mountain, with

---

[1] *Ibid.* p. 314. [2] *Ibid.* pl. xxiii.

[3] Máire MacNeill, *The Festival of Lughanasa. A Study of the Survival of the Celtic Festival of the Beginning of Harvest* (Oxford, 1962), pp. 185–6.

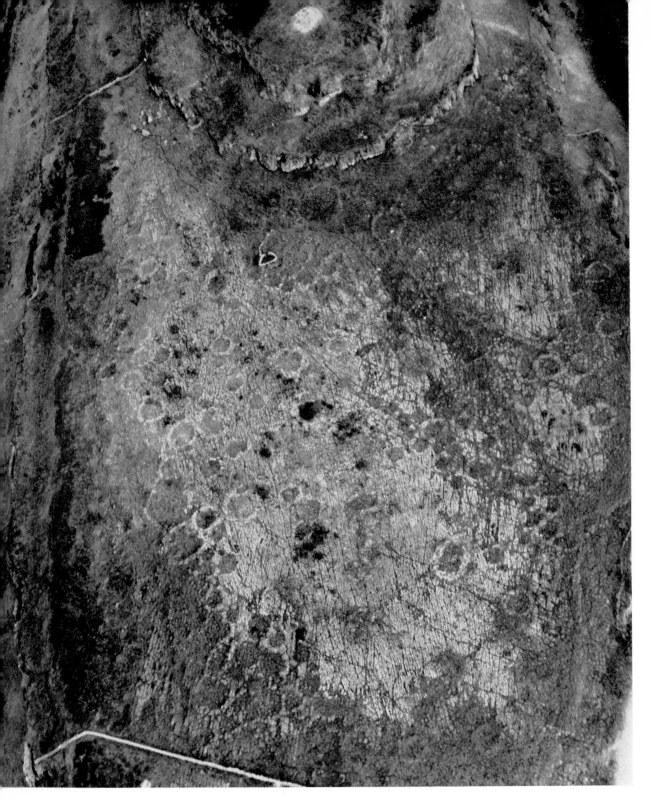

9 'Hut' sites, Bricklieve Mountains, Co. Sligo

traces of human occupation of many ancient periods, but no sign, as at Carrowkeel, of any 'hut' sites. At Knocknashee, also in Co. Sligo, is a steep limestone hill with two cairns. At this place, however, aerial photography has picked out some fifty circular 'hut' sites (fig. 10), 32 feet across in average dimension. These are scattered

10 Cairns and 'huts', Knocknashee, Co. Sligo

along the sheltered eastern side of the hill, at the same altitude as the cairns. The structures, now turf-covered, are quite distinct, but are strikingly similar to those at Carrowkeel. Perhaps these, too, were built when the hillside was bare rock, and perhaps many more examples remain beneath the turf—both here and else-where—awaiting discovery. Are these curious circular enclosures to be thought of as the shelters or dwellings of the Megalithic peoples who built the nearby cairns?

Most remarkable and most celebrated, of course, are the three huge tombs—New-grange, Dowth and Knowth—which surmount the glacial hillocks on the north bank of the Boyne in Co. Meath. The bend of the river stretches across an area of five miles, and here are almost forty prehistoric monuments of various types. Many more must once have existed; aerial photography has already managed to identify several circular cropmarks indicating sites as yet unknown. Plainly the whole area must originally have been invested with immense religious and social significance. But apart from some raths, probably of the late Iron Age, all the remains in the Bend of the Boyne seem to have had burial or ritual purpose. The actual dwellings of the Megalithic people who built this passage-grave cemetery have not been found. 'We do not know', as Mrs O'Kelly has recently written, 'who built the Boyne tombs nor who were interred in them.'[1] All that can with certainty be said is that they were a group of Megalithic people and that their great mounds cover passage-graves of striking technical achievement. Radio-carbon dating has suggested that these graves were, like known continental examples, constructed between 3,000 and 2,500 B.C. But that is about as far as it is possible to go with any measure of accuracy.[2] Even the religious beliefs of these peoples, which inspired such impressive undertakings, are entirely lost. It is only certain that they subscribed to survival after death, for the grave-goods included with the remains in most Irish Megalithic tombs were items presumably useful to the deceased in their new lives. The very existence of these monuments, however, the high skills evident in their construction, the social organisation upon which the builders depended, the means of bringing both materials and labour to the site, and the artistic decorations found on so many of the slabs—all these things confirm the high measure of sophistication and the economic well-being of the Megalithic people. 'It becomes more and more evident', Mrs O'Kelly has remarked, 'that the building of Newgrange was no trial-and-error, hit-and-miss affair, but the work of practised builders who fully appreciated the factors which would best assure long life for their monument.'[3] Newgrange itself, with its 62-foot-long passage and cruciform-shaped, corballed-roof chamber, and its gigantic covering cairn of small stones carried up from the Boyne, was the first of these monuments to be explored. Its contents, indeed, like that of the other tombs in the area, were rifled at many points in the past. New excavations begun by Professor O'Kelly in 1962 are still in progress. The line of decorated kerb-stones surrounding the mound (its perimeter is over 300 yards) has been exposed, and two small satellite mounds have been shown to contain passage-graves. There are several other passage-graves within a half-mile radius. Newgrange is still 45 feet high and must once have been higher—before local farmers, over several centuries, used the stones for field banks. White quartzite pebbles, presumably carried from the Wicklow Mountains or from Co. Tyrone, were once heaped upon the side of the cairn around the entrance to the chamber. Twelve standing stones remain to indicate that a circle of these large uprights once surrounded the mound. Such a feature has no counterpart at other Irish passage-graves.

The Dowth mound is about the same size as Newgrange: 280 feet in diameter and 47 feet high. It contains two passage-graves, both of which are roofed with capstones. Some of the slabs are decorated. A souterrain of late date—perhaps of the early

[1] Clair O'Kelly, *Newgrange* (Wexford, 1967), p. 21.   [2] Ó Ríordáin and Daniel, *Newgrange*, p. 132.
[3] O'Kelly, *Newgrange*, p. 79.

11 Excavations at Knowth, Co. Meath

Christian period—was also found in the mound. There are at least five small passage-graves in the area. At Knowth the mound is also about 100 yards in diameter. Excavations begun by Dr Eogan in 1962 are still in progress, and fig. 11 shows the work as it was in the summer of 1967. It is hoped to uncover $6\frac{1}{2}$ acres of ground eventually, in order to establish not only that the site was important in many prehistoric periods but that the great mound is the focal point of a whole complex of passage-graves.[1] In this it is proving similar to both Newgrange and Dowth, the other foci of the huge Boyne cemetery. By the end of 1967 about two-thirds of the perimeter of the Knowth mound had been uncovered, and eight of the ten smaller Megalithic graves in the immediate area had been excavated. Six of these satellite mounds proved to be certain passage-graves; the other two were too ruined for their type to be determined. These smaller sites can be seen in the photograph, grouped around the great mound. There may be still more of these graves awaiting discovery,

[1] George Eogan, 'The Knowth Excavations', in *Antiquity*, XLI (1967), 302.

27

since in some cases known examples had been almost entirely levelled.[1] The excavation of the great mound has revealed its careful and skilful construction. Layers of turf, clay, small stones and shale were put down so that each gradually thickened towards the centre. This method minimised slipping and subsidence. Quartzite pebbles have been found mixed with the débris around the tomb entrance, and this seems to imply that they were used for decorative or symbolic purpose on that side of the mound, as at Newgrange. Many of the Knowth kerb-stones and orthostats are decorated. The passage itself extends inwards from the western face to a distance of 113 feet; the roof of the chamber has capstones, not corbelling. Excavation of the chamber has not yet begun, but fragments of cremated bone have been seen there.[2]

Large earthen circular or oval enclosures are sometimes associated with pre-historic burials. In Ireland no dating has yet been established. The largest of these monuments, like the Longstone Rath in Co. Kildare, the Giant's Ring at Ballynahatty in Co. Down, and the circle at Dowth in the Boyne cemetery, form a distinct type; but their exact date and function are obscure. Dowth has an inner ditch, like the henge monuments of Britain, but the other examples do not. The Giant's Ring at Ballynahatty (fig. 12), encloses an area of 7 acres. The bank, which is over 60 feet wide, still rises to a height of 12 feet. This earthwork is built upon a gravel terrace and the bank was constructed of subsoil and gravel removed from the interior of the enclosure. This created an internal shallow depression. A section excavated in 1954 showed that there had never been an inner ditch.[3] The bank has five entrances, but none of these formed 'opposed entrances' of the henge type—like those of the Dowth circle—and it is not even certain that they were part of the original design.[4] Slightly to the east of the centre of the enclosed area is a single-chambered Megalithic tomb, with five orthostats and a capstone. The covering cairn has been destroyed. The purpose of the Giant's Ring remains unclear. The 1954 excavations found slight evidence of occupation—charcoal, and many worked flints. A late Neolithic date seems about right. But the earthwork cannot have been a dwelling area, and its construction and function were probably in accordance with ritual needs. As with some British 'henge' monuments, a large number of burials have been found nearby, in fields to the north, where nineteenth-century ploughing revealed numerous simple cist graves. But of the ritual performed at this place no knowledge is possible, though its funereal implications are inescapable. In 1938 an aerial photograph recorded a similar though smaller circle on the bank of the Boyne, 800 yards to the south of Newgrange. The monument—long since flattened by

---

[1] George Eogan, 'A New Passage-Grave in Co. Meath', in *Antiquity*, XXXVII (1963), 226.
[2] Eogan, *Antiquity*, XLI, 303.
[3] A.E.P. Collins, 'Excavations at the Giant's Ring', in *U.J.A.* XX (1957), 44. (See also a plan of the ring on p. 45.) See also, *An Archaeological Survey of Co. Down* (H.M.S.O., 1966) pp. 89–91.
[4] *Ibid.* p. 49.

12 Giant's Ring, Ballynahatty, Co. Down

ploughing[1]—appeared partly as a cropmark and partly as an extremely low, levelled earthwork (fig. 13). It has been picked out by aerial photographs on several subsequent years and may even be seen, once that attention has been drawn to it, from the top of the Newgrange mound. Clearly the bank was formerly very large, but there is no sign of a ditch. It is difficult to say whether there was ever an entrance: the southeastern part of the bank is the most levelled, and a slight deflection of the circle at this point suggests the site of an entrance. Stones scattered over the nearby field surface, may not have come from the monument at all, but may have belonged to much later field boundaries.[2] Probably this circle was a ritual enclosure intimately

[1] It is not marked on the 1837 Ordnance Survey maps.
[2] S. P. Ó Ríordáin, 'Unrecorded Earthwork near Newgrange', in *J.R.S.A.I.* LXXXIV (1954), 93.

13 Cropmarks of a 'ring monument' near Newgrange, Co. Meath

related to the burial customs of the great passage-grave cemetery within which it is situated.

During the centuries in which the Megalithic people were building their huge tombs a slow economic revolution was taking place. The Bronze Age in Ireland was not the result of any invasions or settlements: the Megalithic people, and the Neolithic farmers among whom they had settled, adopted new techniques of metal-working brought across to them from Iberia, and between 2,000 and 1,700 B.C. they had learnt to alloy copper with tin. Most Irish copper-ores were to be found in the south-western coastal regions, and most of the tin was imported from Cornwall, although small placer deposits in the Wicklow Mountains were almost certainly worked. The rich deposits of alluvial gold in the Vale of Avoca and adjoining streams, once thay had been identified, were exploited on an increasing scale, so that the Wicklow Mountains became one of the principal sources of gold in western Europe, and led to a long-distance trade in Irish bronze and gold objects. Irish gold ornaments of this period have been found in many parts of Britain. The Irish Bronze Age was a time of apparent domestic peace and of considerable technical advance. At first, and indeed for a long time, the use of metal must have been restricted to the wealthy. Domestic and agricultural implements of wood and stone continued in use alongside metal throughout prehistoric times—and, indeed, into the middle ages. But in the Bronze Age advances in trade and communication were especially marked. They indicate a high degree of agricultural efficiency, too, since the mining and trading elements in the community must have owed their existence to an agricultural surplus of production.[1] By the later Bronze Age there is evidence that long-distance trade routes had developed still more. Amber from the Baltic and faience beads (manufactured in Egypt after about 1,500 B.C.) are often found in the country, no doubt imported in exchange for Irish gold. Our knowledge about the dwelling places of this period is extremely shadowy. Small 'cabins' of the Lough Gur type were probably most typical, and the earliest crannógs were being built—though these were still rare. Of agricultural organisation and field systems nothing is known. Burial customs yield most of our information about the Bronze Age.

The types of funeral monument constructed throughout the period demonstrate a considerable stability. The simple cist burials, for the less distinguished members of society, are the most typical both of this period and of the succeeding Iron Age. Burials in these 'cists'—box-like structures formed of stone slabs—were single, one person per cist. Most Bronze Age cists were for cremations and the tombs were small; the ubiquitous 'short cists'. The 'long cists', usually for inhumation, are more typically of later date, and most early Christian burials are of this sort. Beaker-ware food vessels and other grave-goods often give some indication of the period of a cist burial. Occasionally cists were grouped together and a low cairn, surrounded by kerb-stones, was built over them. More frequently the cists were simply buried in the earth and the site possibly marked by a wooden pillar. Tall standing-stones, like the famous one at Punchestown in Co. Kildare, were occasionally erected over cist graves of the early Bronze Age. Again, cremated remains were sometimes just buried in an urn, without a monument of any kind. 'Ring-barrows' were also common throughout the country, but most particularly in the lowland areas which were later intensively exploited by agriculture, so that the majority of barrows have been levelled. They were low mounds, about 15 to 30 feet in diameter, formed by digging a circular ditch and heaping the earth into the centre over a simple cist or unprotected burial. Most examples are of Bronze Age date, although late Neolithic pottery was

---

[1] Raftery, *Prehistoric Ireland*, p. 136.

14 Cropmarks of ring-barrows, near Lisduff Bridge, Co. Tipperary

found in the ring-barrows at Rathjordan in Co. Limerick.[1] Some however, fall within the early Iron Age. Ring-barrows are quite commonly grouped together on low-lying ground. Near Lisduff Bridge, in Co. Tipperary—an area where there are many concentrations—a whole cemetery of ploughed-out barrows have been seen as crop-marks in a field (fig. 14).[2] The sites of the barrows are now indicated by small circular ditches which yielded the material for the mounds. Of the burials themselves nothing now remains; at some time in the past the graves must have been broken into by the plough. Much less numerous than the simple ring-barrows were the so-called

[1] Ó Ríordáin, *Antiquities of the Irish Countryside*, p. 79.
[2] The straight lines defining old field boundaries also show as cropmarks. Their orientation differs from that of the modern fields

15   Cropmarks of a bell-barrow and a cist burial, near Castledermot, Co. Kildare

'bell-barrows'. In these a space was left between the burial mound and the ditch, or, more rarely, the two ditches which surrounded it. Fig. 15 shows the circular ring-ditch cropmark at the site of what is almost certainly a ploughed-out 'bell-barrow' in the corner of a field some 3 miles to the north-east of Castledermot in Co. Kildare. Close to it, and now also appearing as a circular cropmark, was a simple mound, probably covering a cist burial.

Sometime after about 1,200 B.C. a series of new external influences began to reach Ireland, bringing about distinct cultural changes in the late Bronze Age. New types of domestic implements and weapons appear, and these fresh influences became diffused fairly evenly throughout the country. In burial customs and therefore, presumably, in religion, there were no discernible alterations, and, it must be assumed that the late Bronze Age cultural diversifications were prompted by trading links with northern European lands rather than by any new movements of peoples. At some unknown point there was another innovation: the use of iron. The European Iron Age had begun shortly after 1,000 B.C., and by the sixth century B.C. was widely established and had certainly reached Britain. Probably the first iron working began in Ireland quite soon after that. Since late Bronze Age culture was so sensitive to external influences it is difficult to suppose that iron technology was not adopted at an early date. Yet its adoption must have been slow and was almost certainly at first highly regional. Nevertheless by about the fifth century B.C. the Irish Iron Age had begun: it lasted until the eleventh century A.D., and in a few isolated areas Iron Age culture lingered until long after that. (The division between the Early and Late Iron Age is conventionally drawn during the fifth century A.D.,[1] when the country was Christianised, and prehistory gave place to history as Latin culture was introduced by the Church.) Bronze Age society in Ireland was just absorbing the new metallurgical techniques when fresh immigrants began to arrive in the country. Their coming considerably accelerated economic change.

The Celts were a vigorous people from Central Europe whose expansion by the third century B.C., had brought them south to Italy, east to the Black Sea, and north and west to Britain and to Ireland. The Irish version of Celtic La Tène artistic styles can first be noticed in the third century B.C., but at that early time Celtic influences were still comparatively minor, and Bronze Age culture predominated. Certainly by 150 B.C. the Celtic peoples were well-established in Ireland, and from this stage their influence began to spread fairly evenly throughout the country. A syncretism in part occurred. 'There were, indeed, accretions to the cultural content,' Dr Raftery has written; 'but at no stage can one discern in the archaeological record such an overwhelming cultural change as to allow of the interpretation that one population was completely submerged in another new one, or completely destroyed by it.'[2] This is a conservative assessment, even as far as the archaeological evidence is concerned; and in language, law, and religion—in fact in the whole organisation of society—it is clear that Ireland became thoroughly Celtic during the Early Iron Age. And since the Romans never extended their dominion or influence over the country, Ireland preserved and transmitted the institutions of the Celtic world to historical times. Before the Romans began to withdraw from their British provinces, the Irish ('Scots') expanded into their western fringes. During the fourth and fifth centuries they colonised Cornwall, south and north Wales, the Isle of Man, and the western

[1] S. P. Ó Ríordáin, 'Prehistory in Ireland, 1937–46', in *P.P.S.* XIII (1947), 163.
[2] *The Celts*, ed. by Joseph Raftery (The Thomas Davis Lectures, 1960), (Cork, 1967 edition), p. 47.

coastal regions of Scotland.[1] The Celts had first arrived in Ireland in successive waves, and there is no evidence to relate whether they came as conquerors or as more peaceful immigrants. Three distinct ethnic groups seem to have settled: the Cruthin (in the north-east of the country), the Érainn (in the south-east and south-west), and the Goídil (in the central areas). The Goídil were the Celts who came to predominate, and it was rival Goídil princes who eventually ruled from the main centres.[2] Ptolemy's map of Ireland, which dates from the mid-second century A.D., gives Celtic names for the tribes who lived near the southern and eastern coasts.[3]

There are descriptions of Celtic society in Ireland as it was towards the close of the Early Iron Age. The epic tales were handed down in the form of oral tradition and eventually written down by later Christian monks, but they were probably composed in about the fourth century A.D. The characters of the heroic literature were certainly mythological and their exploits fictional; but the society described is a real one,[4] and the setting of warfare along the frontier between the Ulster kingdom and the men of Connacht is historical. There are also valuable indications about the structure of Celtic Iron Age society in the law tracts, some of which were written down as early as the seventh century. These, uninfluenced by Roman law, preserved ancient Indo-European legal and social concepts. Archaeological evidence of course can provide much information about this society, although it is quite often of a very limited scope. It can usually give a clear picture of actual living conditions, although as far as burials are concerned, there seems to have been little departure from Bronze Age custom except for the increasing tendency to 'long cist' burials. Aerial photography, too, can furnish us with useful evidence by picking out the structure of the Celtic Iron Age from a countryside littered with remains of earlier and later date. Their raths, their crannógs, and their distinctive hill and promontory forts are still to be seen incised upon the surface of the ground.

The people who built these places were ruled over by petty regional kings, themselves subject to over-kings. There is no clear picture of this political structure until the historical period of the late Iron Age, but it is evident both from the epic literature and from the surviving linear defensive earthworks (like the Black Pig's Dyke and the Dane's Cast) that the northern kingdom of Ulster, ruled from Emain Macha (the existing Navan Rath near Armagh), enjoyed considerable prestige and much actual power in the last centuries of the Early Iron Age. Its chief rival in the epic literature was the Connacht Kingdom (whose capital at Cruachain—Rathcroghan—in Co. Roscommon, also still exists). To the south lay the kingdom of Leinster about

[1] Ibid. pp. 75 ff.
[2] Myles Dillon and Nora K. Chadwick, The Celtic Realms (London, 1967), p. 5.
[3] Ibid. p. 19, and Raftery, Prehistoric Ireland, p. 214.
[4] Kenneth Jackson, The Oldest Irish Tradition: A Window on the Iron Age, (The Rede Lecture, 1964), (Cambridge, 1964), p. 44.

which very little is known during this period. In the fifth century A.D., however, new dynastic arrangements introduced a revised territorial structure of government. The boundaries of the Ulster Kingdom were driven back and only a small fragment of it remained in the extreme north-east. The victor was the first definitely known historical ruler: Niall of the Nine Hostages. His descendants established the great Uí Néill dynasty, which governed most of the northern and midland kingdoms. In the fifth century, the south of Ireland was under the hegemony of the Eóchanacht dynasty which, despite some friction with its northern neighbours, seems to have enjoyed long interludes of peace, and to have attained considerable wealth and social stability. Thus by the end of the fifth century the tradition of five Irish kingdoms had certainly been ended, and by the seventh and eighth centuries, when ecclesiastical literary evidence is available, the country had completely fragmented. The great over-kings had very limited authority, and Ireland emerged into historical times divided into about 150 *tuatha* (or petty local kingdoms). Their dwellings were merely substantial raths. The laws required a king to live in a rath with bank and ditch,[1] and the multivallate raths presumably belonged to the more important kings. It is true that surviving examples of multivallate raths, and the cropmark indications of still more recently discovered by aerial photography, amount to a number hugely in excess of 150. But raths were frequently deserted and new settlements made on fresh ground, and the figure of 150 *tuatha* is probably about right. The petty kings paid tribute to an over-king, but the over-kings had no authority in the domestic affairs of the *tuatha* under them. The Uí Néill rulers continued to assume the titles of the kingdom of Tara, but in reality they lived in a style scarcely different from the petty rulers around them. Yet despite this political devolution, the cultural unity of Ireland remained intact. Language, law, and art were uniform: so was religion, both before and after the conversion of the country to Christianity.

Within society distinctions were well-defined. Individuals *per se* enjoyed no rights; rights resulted from a man's membership of a *fine* or 'joint-family'. All landownership was vested in the *fine*, and only freemen could participate in it. There were also unfree men and slaves: they are scarcely mentioned in the epic tales.[2] Social status was imparted both by inheritance and by acquired riches. The *fili*, for example, and later the Christian clergy, were highly placed; a lawyer of the highest grade was equal in status with the ruler of a *tuath*. Social mobility was also encouraged by provisions which allowed unfree men to aquire status by learning and practising a skilled trade. The economy of this society was largely pastoral. Trade and exchange-value were expressed in terms of cattle and the *cumul* (female slave)—there was no native Irish coinage until the Norman period.[3] Agricultural

---

[1] *Críth Gablach*, ed. D. A. Binchy (Dublin, 1941), ll. 566–72.
[2] *Ibid.* p. 11. [3] Dillon and Chadwick, *Celtic realms*, p. 108.

36

organisation is rather obscure, though fields of the Iron Age period have shown up on aerial photographs and are discussed later.[1] Archaeological finds suggest a range of domestic goods only appropriate to communities of considerable prosperity. Some sort of contact with Roman Britain was probably maintained, although there is, again, little firm information about this. Roman coins and silverware have been found in Ireland, but it is likely that they were the spoils brought back after Irish raids across the sea. The religious beliefs and practices of the Iron Age appear to differ little from Celtic religion elsewhere—in Gaul, for example. The Celts believed in the transmigration of the individual soul, and they supposed that certain rivers and woodlands were sacred. Their gods tended to dwell in isolation and some were thought to live underground. The great Megalithic tombs, which were over two thousand years old when the Celtic peoples came to Ireland, were held in especial veneration. They were believed to be the homes of gods. Whoever robbed the Boyne tombs of their contents, it cannot have been the early Celts. These people were cruel and artistic, boastful and skilled. Yet they seem, strangely, to have found in Christianity something which was sufficiently familiar to enable their conversion to take place with comparative ease. There were no martyrs in Ireland: society was claimed for Christ without bloodshed.

The surviving traces of this Iron Age civilisation lie upon the Irish countryside in almost chaotic profusion. The dwellings, the fortresses, and (after the conversion) the monastic houses, are still evident everywhere. In the following chapters these remains are considered in broad perspective—as they are seen by the aerial photographer: a part of the changing landscape.

[1] See ch. 3.

3

IRON AGE DWELLINGS AND FIELDS

OF ALL THE REMAINS of early Irish society, the circular earthworks known as raths are by far the most common. They are scattered across the countryside with such regularity as to give a first appearance—though a false one—of having been deliberately established according to a scheme of planned distances. Panoramas of the Irish Lowlands, like that to the north of Granard in Co. Longford (fig. 16), usually show at least a couple of surviving raths. Throughout Ireland generally, there are probably considerably more than thirty thousand of them. Many others have been destroyed, and now survive only in the names of villages and townlands. Some which existed when the first Ordnance Survey was completed in the first half of the nineteenth century, and are there marked as 'forts', are no longer in existence.[1] Most of these vanished raths were destroyed by agriculture, or, in the case of those banks which were reinforced with stone, to provide materials for the building of field-boundaries, roads and houses. Banks have been levelled and ditches filled in ever since the raths were first built; there is evidence that many were only occupied for quite short periods before their desertion led to decay. Quite a large number of destroyed raths can be rediscovered from the air in terms of cropmarks, giving a clearer picture of the plan of a rath than can ever be obtained from surviving examples, with eroded ramparts and infilled ditches.

Although they are frequently described as 'ring-forts', Irish raths in fact had a domestic purpose: they were the homes of farmers. The largest examples were the dwelling-places of the most substantial farmers of the community—the local chieftains. They are not of very early date. There is no evidence that any were constructed before the Iron Age, and the vast number seem to coincide with the late Iron Age and early Christian period—between the fifth and the eleventh centuries. Evidence from the comparatively few raths so far excavated seems to point to that period. Lissue rath, in Co. Antrim, excavated by Dr Bersu, proved to be early ninth century in date.[2] It had already been deserted before the end of the tenth century. In Cork several raths are dated to the fifth, sixth, and seventh centuries by rare finds of pottery.[3] At Dressograth in Co. Antrim, Neolithic (but no Bronze Age) material was

---

[1] E. E. Evans and M. Gaffikin, 'Megaliths and Raths', in *Irish Naturalists' Journal*, V (1935), 242.

[2] Gerhard Bersu, 'The Rath in Townland Lissue, Co. Antrim. Report on Excavations in 1946', in *U.J.A.* X (1947), 57.

[3] V. B. Proudfoot, 'The Economy of an Irish Rath', in *Medieval Archaeology*, V (1961), 97.

16   The Black Pig's Dyke north of Granard, Co. Longford, looking north-west

found during recent excavations, but this seems only to point to an earlier occupation of the site. The rath itself belongs to the Early Christian period.[1] Raths continued to be built and occupied until comparatively late periods—certainly in post-Norman times, and some as late as the seventeenth, and even the nineteenth centuries,[2] and without excavation it is impossible to say whether a particular earthwork is early or late. Some of the very earliest examples, even after exploration, still cannot be dated unambiguously. The famous rath complex at Cush, Co. Limerick, has been assigned

[1] A. E. P. Collins, 'Excavations at Dressograth Rath, Co. Antrim', in *U.J.A.* XIX (1966), 217.
[2] Evans, *Prehistoric and Early Christian Ireland*, p. 28.

17   Earthworks at Slieve Breagh, Co. Meath

to the late Bronze Age on the basis of some finds of that period: but it seems probable
that the raths date only from the third century B.C. at the very earliest, and that the
Bronze Age burials found on the site existed long before the raths, whose builders,
indeed, were ignorant of their existence.[1] A similar site in many respects occurs at
Slieve Breagh in Co. Meath (fig. 17). On this hill, quite undisturbed by agriculture,
are the remains of no less than thirty-two earthworks, some faint and some distinct.
They appear to be a very early type of rath. Most have circular banks with inner
ditches, and entrances formed by gaps in the banks. Some are conjoined, and some

[1] Proudfoot, 'Economy of an Irish Rath', p. 97.

have slightly raised interiors, like the later 'platform raths'. The earthworks seem to have served various purposes: a few for burial, and a large number for dwelling. They have been provisionally dated to either the late Bronze Age or the early Iron Age.[1]

Rath settlements of the characteristic, late Iron Age, period occurred on comparatively low-lying ground—on sands and gravels, and on the tops of drumlins.[2] Uplands and heavy clay country were avoided. The occupation of the builders dictated the choice of sites: they were primarily cattlemen, attracted to rich pasture lands. They also grew vegetables and flax. Discoveries of storage-pits, kilns for drying grain and quern-stones associated with raths establish that corn was cultivated even if only over a small area surrounding the farmstead. A heavy iron plough was used. Many finds of iron ore and slag point to a domestic smelting industry. But the economy was mainly pastoral: a man's status was measured by his clients and by the number of his cattle.

There is considerable variation in the size of raths. Some of the very smallest examples, only 30 or 50 feet in diameter, probably served as cattle enclosures or as the homes of poor men. Most of those which contained a dwelling are 100 to 150 feet in diameter, and there are some very large ones—200 to 300 feet.[3] The circular enclosing banks of a typical rath farmstead must originally have been quite high; some may even have been topped by a palisade in the form of wooden stakes, although erosion of the highest part of the banks inhibits the survival of archaeological evidence for this.[4] The ditches were deep enough to form a serious obstacle, and on low-lying sites a few may have been filled with water. The original depth of the ditch can usually be determined by the careful removal of accumulated layers of earth and stones. Except for some of the very large and rather more complicated examples, however, it is doubtful that the earthworks of farmstead raths were defensive in purpose. They are much more likely to have been constructed as a means of keeping animals in, and wild beasts out. Cattle-raiding was the most commonplace diversion in early Irish society—as the literature describes at immense length—and the impressive earthen walls of raths were doubtless a protection against thieves who might drive off freely wandering animals at night. Ditches customarily occur outside the rampart, but where they are within they may have contained water for the animals, or they may, alternatively, as Ó Ríordáin suggested, have been of ritual significance.[5]

A typical rath of average size is Lismore Fort, near Smarmore, Co. Louth (fig. 18). This has one earthen rampart and one external ditch—now filled in. Agriculture has

[1] Liam de Paor and Marcus P. Óh-Eochaidhe, 'Unusual Group of Earthworks at Slieve Breagh, Co. Meath', in *J.R.S.A.I.* LXXXVI (1956), p. 101.
[2] O. Davies, 'Types of Rath in Southern Ulster', in *U.J.A.* X (1947), 2.
[3] T. J. Westropp, 'The Ancient Forts of Ireland', in *T.R.I.A.* XXXI (1902), 588.
[4] Ó Ríordáin, *Antiquities of the Irish Countryside*, p. 5.   [5] *Ibid.* p. 11.

18 Simple rath: Lismore Fort, Smarmore, Co. Louth

destroyed any further earthworks which may once have existed, and today even the centre of the rath is used for growing crops. The entrance gateway, once probably flanked by large posts, now appears as a gap in the rampart. Such simple univallate raths can be found in thousands throughout the countryside, and even those which have been sacrificed to the plough may still reappear when under favourable crops. Two miles south-west of Kilkeel, Co. Down, for example, a destroyed univallate rath is seen again in terms of cropmarks in a field of wheat (fig. 19). The mark in fact denotes the ditch infilled with humus-rich soil, there lying to a greater depth than over the surrounding land. One half of the rath is visible; the remainder of the

19 Cropmarks of a rath near Kilkeel, Co. Down

site lies, beyond a hedge, in two fields also under cultivation, but no cropmarks appear. The gateway is clearly defined in the half which is visible. Its appearance as a gap in the ditch signifies that the rath-builders left a short unexcavated sector for the entrance. On some sites, however, the ditch is a complete circle, an entrance being made subsequently by adding a causeway across it.

The single, univallate rath was the most common structure in the early Irish countryside, belonging to a society where there were no villages, but only isolated farmsteads. More elaborate multivallate raths were also quite plentiful. These circular earthworks were of essentially the same construction and fulfilled the same purpose. In typical examples, the diameter of the enclosed area might also vary, but instead of a bank and single ditch there might be two or three ditches. These addi-

20   Trivallate rath near Ballymote, Co. Sligo

tional earthworks were not intended as a supplement to defence, but were a symbolical indication of better social standing.[1] According to tradition, the rath of a king should have a double rampart at least—the outer earthworks being constructed by the humblest vassals as a form of tribute. Fig. 20 shows a typical trivallate rath which lies four miles south of Ballymote in Co. Sligo, an area especially rich in such settlements. Fig. 21 illustrates a comparable example where the outer earthworks have been entirely destroyed by agriculture, but the plan can be traced nevertheless with great clarity in terms of cropmarks (fig. 21). A mounded area within the original central enclosure still appears; this probably indicates the house site, and is now overgrown with small shrubs. It lies in a field some 1½ miles to the south-west of

[1] Evans, *Prehistoric and Early Christian Ireland*, p. 25.

21 Cropmarks of a trivallate rath, near Muine Bheagh, Co. Carlow

Muine Bheagh in Co. Carlow. The dark circles indicate the site of the triple ditches. Three miles to the north-west of Dundalk, at Kilcurry (fig. 22), another cropmark has revealed the position of a large bivallate rath. A circular dwelling adjoins the inside bank: its entrance is still clearly visible. There are possible traces of two other internal house sites. The rath itself has an elaborate entrance, and there are additional cropmarks of field boundaries all round the site. The position of the chief circular house within the rath is seen as a growth of crop lighter in tone than that on the surrounding ground: there has been differential response in the crop to layers of occupation débris.

22 Cropmarks of a rath near Dundalk, Co. Louth

Almost all Irish raths are circular: exceptions, which are rare, include a few in eastern parts of the country that are square or rectangular, besides several D-shaped examples. None of these have yet been excavated, and it is not unlikely that many of them may turn out to be of post-Norman date.[1] The actual dwellings of a rath were nearly always within the enclosure. An enclosure as much as 120 feet in diameter

[1] For a recent list of excavated raths, see Proudfoot, 'Economy of an Irish Rath', p. 119. He gives the total number as forty-seven.

46

provided room enough for several houses or storage huts. These often stood within the western side of the enclosure so as to gain maximum shelter from the wind. Houses were customarily circular, but sometimes square-shaped. They were of wood and can sometimes be detected archaeologically by the discovery of the post-holes of the timbers which once supported the roof. Destruction by fire usually leaves in the soil a dark stain of charred wood, which may still be traced by excavation. But post-holes and charcoal deposits frequently present a confusing appearance, for during the occupation of a rath there was often much re-building, and interpretation of remains now seen as confused and overlapping layers may not be easy. In his excavation of the Lissue rath, Dr Bersu found a large number of post-holes, indicating where buildings had been constantly reconstructed.[1] Yet he considered that there was sufficient evidence to support his conjecture—widely disputed—that a single roof of wattles covered the entire rath, like those in the Isle of Man.[2] Building mutations and the other accumulations of habitation tended to raise the interior levels of some raths slightly above surrounding land. This, and the occasional addition of fresh soil to the interior, explains the 'platform raths' which are so common. No doubt the dwellers heaped on fresh soil as a means of cleaning the inside of an enclosure which must have become littered with bones and refuse, and thereby postponing a move—otherwise clearly frequent enough, in view of the huge number of raths—to an entirely new site.

Two other features require special mention. Entrance gateways were sometimes very elaborate, usually with wooden doors attached to large side-posts (gateway post-holes survive in several excavated examples). Stone gateways to earthen raths, sometimes with lintels, were not frequent, but did occur. Stone was much more commonly used in facing the earthen banks, and in the construction of souterrains. These subterranean passages (often known as 'caves' in the countryside, and so marked on maps) were excavated so that their entrances opened from the floor of a house. They are very commonly found in Irish raths. The purpose of souterrains is obscure: they were probably not essentially for defence, though some contain built-in traps and snags to deter an intruder. Despite the polished surfaces of the stone walls in some examples, suggesting the frequent passage of cattle, it is unlikely that they were used as animal shelters except, perhaps, in times of danger. Chimneys and chambers in the more ambitious souterrains point to occasional temporary habitation. But probably their primary use was for storage.

Inside a rath the foundation of a house can sometimes still be distinctly seen. At Rathealy, three miles south-west of Freshford in Co. Kilkenny (fig. 23), the house sites are especially clear. This large trivallate rath contains the visible remains of a rectangular house, a circular house, and the entrance of a souterrain. But especially

---

[1] Bersu, 'The Rath in Townland Lissue', p. 32.   [2] *Ibid.* p. 45.

23 Rath and associated earthworks at Rathealy, Co. Kilkenny

interesting here are the other earthworks outside the ramparts. The aerial photograph shows two oblong enclosures, one superimposed upon part of the other, indicating rearrangement at some period. These enclosures appear to be contemporary with the rath—whatever its date may have been—and are possibly fields, although their regular shape scarcely suggests this.[1] The remains may, alternatively, be those of a 'street' or 'green'—one of the enclosed and elaborately fenced areas in front of

[1] Proudfoot has remarked upon the comparative absence of early fields associated with raths, but many examples have appeared in the present air survey. (See Proudfoot, 'Economy of an Irish Rath', p. 108.)

48

substantial dwelling-places mentioned in the early literature and used for games.[1] If so, this would prove to be the first known surviving example of such a feature. Further disturbed ground around the rath may mark the remains of either field-boundaries or cattle-enclosures, and even of house sites. A raised mound with an isolated bush by one end marks the site of a medieval church—indicated as a ruin on the first edition of the Ordnance Survey in the 1840's. We know that greens were, at least in some cases, associated with churches.[2] At Carraig Aille, in Co. Limerick, excavation here revealed houses outside the banks of a rath of eighth to eleventh century date.[3]

Some of the larger raths have a loop of wall, forming a crescent-shaped annexe attached to the rampart of the main circular enclosure. These 'double-raths' form a distinct type, and they are not so rare as Dr Davies believed.[4] In most examples, the annexe remains separated from the main rath by the rampart, and has its own bank and ditch and external entrance. It has been suggested that these types are of very late date, and emulate the Norman mote and bailey,[5] but this is very unlikely since there are several which are identifiably of the early period. The large earthwork on the Hill of Uisneach, in Co. Westmeath (fig. 24), is such a double-rath, and of early date. The whole site was exposed during excavations between 1925 and 1928, and after exploration the soil was replaced to preserve the remains. The structure is a large bivallate enclosure, 250 feet across, with dry-stone and earth walls, to which is attached a crescentic annexe, 180 feet across, and a triangular-shaped outwork[6]—probably for cattle. In modern times the rath was denuded of most of its stones for field boundary-walls. The main enclosure is divided into three sections, and one of these is subdivided into three more.[7] There is also a large circular house, 44 feet in diameter, its foundations clearly visible. There were four periods of occupation and the annexe appears to have been added to the western side of the main enclosure during the last of these. Its entrance is a simple gap in the external bank, with a causeway crossing the ditch. There would seem to have been no direct entrance between the annexe and the main rath, but as only the foundations of the dividing wall remain there can be no certainty that a gap did not exist at a higher level in the bank. As well as traces of wooden buildings in the annexe, digging revealed the foundation of a rectangular stone house and a souterrain. These remains invalidate

---

[1] Westropp, 'Ancient Forts of Ireland', p. 664. See also *Táin Bó Cúailnge*, ed. J. Strachan and J. G. O'Keeffe (Dublin, 1912), l. 1240.

[2] *The Monastery of Tallaght*, ed. E. J. Gwynn and W. J. Purton, *P.R.I.A.* xxix (1911).

[3] Ó Ríordáin, *Antiquities of the Irish Countryside*, p. 5.

[4] Davies, 'Types of Rath in Southern Ulster', p. 10. Westropp remarked upon them too; see 'Ancient Forts of Ireland', p. 665.

[5] Davies, 'Types of Rath in Southern Ulster', p. 10.

[6] This feature, discovered during the excavation, is not visible on the photograph.

[7] R. A. S. Macalister and R. Lloyd Praeger, 'Report on the Excavation of Uisneach', in *P.R.I.A.* xxxviii c (1928–9), 85.

24 'Double rath': Hill of Uisneach, Co. Westmeath

the theory that the annexes of double-raths were cattle-enclosures: perhaps the additions were simply a way of enlarging the living space of a rath-community without having to construct a wholly new earthwork in another place. Usually, it is true, the farmers preferred to build a separate rath some distance from the first when more living room was required: but a crescentic annexe is more economical. The Uisneach rath originally appears to have been horsehoe-shaped. For there was no ditch on the western side, and the gap this left was in fact later filled in by the addition of the annexe.[1] During the excavation, several finds seemed to point to the

[1] Macalister and Praeger, 'Report on the Excavation of Uisneach', in *P.R.I.A.* XXXVIIIC (1928-9), p. 97.

25 Cropmarks of a 'double-rath', Clintstown, Co. Kilkenny

voluntary abandonment of the site around A.D. 250. There was no trace of any cultural influence other than of the late La Tène period. Uisneach is, of course, known from annalistic literature as a famous royal site, a seat of the Connaught royal dynasty until the mid-third century. But of its royal associations no trace was found in the excavations, and the rath itself cannot be identified with the royal residence mentioned in the annals.[1]

Chance discoveries of cropmarks provide evidence as to the wide distribution of double-raths, and frequently give a much clearer indication of the original lay-out

[1] *Ibid.* p. 125.

than surviving earthworks. Three miles south of Ballyragget in a field near the banks of the River Nore in Clintstown, Co. Kilkenny, the site of a large double-rath was discovered in aerial reconnaissance (fig. 25). Here the annexe appears to have been enlarged twice, and there are other enclosed areas butting on to the rampart of the main, bivallate enclosure. A horseshoe-shaped house-site is visible inside the main rath; access-ways leading to the settlement can also be seen. Had this rath still existed as an earthwork at the time of the first Ordnance Survey, made during the 1840s, it would surely, in view of its extent, have been marked on the early Ordnance maps. Apart from the chance appearance of the cropmarks, the only surviving evidence for the rath is in the name 'Foulkesrath' castle, a nearby house, now a youth hostel, which dates back to at least the fifteenth century. In size and plan, the Clintstown cropmark rath was probably not unlike Dron Castle, a huge bivallate double-rath near Ballymore, Westmeath.

Double-raths tend to be very large. Lisnagade Ringfort (Lis na caed), Co. Down (fig. 26), is known as the largest rath in Ireland.[1] It is one of a series of earthworks lying in the eastern shelter of the Dane's Cast—a long defensive bank which, having nothing to do with the Danes, was constructed in the fourth century. Within half a mile of Lisnagade there are ten other raths. The main earthwork at Lisnagade itself is a vast trivallate rath, 370 feet in diameter. To the north lies the most interesting feature: a large annexe linked to a small secondary rath, lying 375 feet away.[2] As at Uisneach, the annexe was used as a living area, and within the second rath are the remains of a square-shaped house and a rectangular structure which might have been a barn.[3] There was much re-building here, and the existing deep ditch is itself a replacement of an earlier, irregular one, the traces of which can still be discerned.

Dry-stone masonry was commonly used by rath-builders to support or to face ramparts. In rocky ground with only a shallow covering of soil, the excavation of ditches and the mounding of earth became too formidable an undertaking, and raths were constructed wholly in stone. These are customarily known as cashels, and are chiefly distributed in the western regions of Ireland and in parts of eastern Ulster. Typically isolated structures like the earthen raths, they, too, were the farmsteads of a society given over to a primarily pastoral economy. None have the close-set walls and ditches characteristic of raths, though many have more widely-spaced outer walls. Mortar was never used in these buildings, but the standard of workmanship in stone was sometimes of the highest. As with raths, no examples can be certainly dated to before the Iron Age.

Perhaps the finest example, and among the most well-known, is Staigue Fort, just

[1] *Archaeological Survey of Northern Ireland, Co. Down* (Belfast, 1966), pp. 149–50.
[2] *A Preliminary Survey of the Ancient Monuments of Northern Ireland*, ed. D. A. Chart (Belfast, 1940), p. 111. *Archaeological Survey of Northern Ireland, Co. Down*, (Belfast, 1966) pp. 149–50.
[3] Proudfoot, 'Economy of an Irish Rath', p. 121.

26 Lisnagade Ringfort, Co. Down

off Kenmare Bay in Co. Kerry (fig. 27). It is built on a mound which is surrounded by a low bank and a shallow ditch. The cashel is 88 feet in diameter, with a wall 13 feet thick at base, sloping inwards to 7 feet at the top. This batter of the wall is a feature of most cashels. An intricate system of ten stairways leads up the inside of the wall to terraces; the wall now varies in height from 10 to 18 feet. There must, originally, have been stone houses within the enclosure. In front of the cashel is a maze of small irregular fields, which are perhaps contemporary with the early occupation of the site. Later field boundaries have been superimposed in one or two places, but modern tillage covers a less extensive area, and this has allowed the

53

27 Staigue Fort, Co. Kerry

earlier field-remains to survive. The date of Staigue is uncertain, but the royal site
of Grianán Aighligh, at Carrowreagh in Co. Donegal is a similar structure where
the period of occupation can at least be fixed between the fifth and the twelfth
centuries. As the seat of the kings of the Northern Uí Néill the site is frequently
referred to in the *Annals*. In 676 it was dismantled by the Southern Uí Néill, and in
1101 was again destroyed, this time by the King of Munster. The cashel has three
outer rings of wall occupying over five acres. The main circular structure has terraced
walls and staircases, and inside is the foundation of a square house. But the building
is much cruder than Staigue, and is, moreover, a sort of text-book example of poor

54

restoration. The cashel was virtually a heap of stones, 6 feet high, when Dr Walter Bernard began his work of reconstruction in 1873. The walls, when he had finished, were some 17 feet high but with variations; for, as the restorer wrote at the time, 'at first we made the entire structure uniform in height, but looking at it from a distance it was found unsightly'. And as he also remarked, 'the men in rebuilding this had nothing to guide them but the eye, and took the greatest possible pains to imitate the structure and inclination of the original'.[1] The result is that the existing upper terraces and stairways in the batter walls are all of nineteenth-century origin.

Leacanabuaile, near Caherciveen in Co. Kerry, a much smaller cashel was, like so many others, built upon a rocky outcrop. Over the years the walls had collapsed and the whole ruin had become covered with soil. After excavation in 1939–40 the site was left exposed for permanent display, and now presents a clear picture of a typical small farmstead of the early period. Excavation revealed an enclosing wall, 10 feet thick at base, with a rubble core between faces of dressed stone. Ten flights of steps lead up the inside of the wall. A gateway on the eastern side of the enclosure may once have had lintels.[2] Even before excavation the outlines of two stone houses could be seen within the cashel, and digging exposed the low walls of two more; beneath them were the traces of several earlier houses, indicating extensive reconstructions during the periods of occupation. The visible remains are of a clochán, communicating with a rectangular house with post-holes in the floor, two roughly square-shaped dwellings built against the inside walls of the cashel, and the traces of two other clochán. There is also a souterrain and a wall-chamber. The clochán appear to be the oldest structures, but the souterrain and wall-chamber are demonstrably contemporary with the main ramparts since they depend upon them structurally. Objects discovered during the excavation suggest occupation around the fifth or sixth centuries. As in nearly all other excavated examples, no pottery was found, and the inhabitants would seem to have used wooden vessels. Similar in size, but with much less substantial walls (and therefore more typical), is the cashel at Ballynavenooragh near Kilmalkedar in Co. Kerry (fig. 28). There are four ruined clochán within the enclosing wall. Here the site chosen was not a rock outcrop, it lies near the foot of a gentle slope on the edge of the coastal plain.

The Aran Islands contain a large group of especially well-preserved stone 'forts', which still relate to the surrounding countryside as they must anciently have done. Dún Conor, built upon the edge of a low ridge (fig. 29), commands the whole of Inishmaan. This huge cashel measures (internally) 226 feet by 115, with an oval enclosing wall 18 feet thick at the base and 20 feet high—impressive enough by any

---

[1] Walter Bernard, 'Exploration and Restoration of the Ruin of the Grianan of Aileach', in *P.R.I.A.* I (1879), 417.

[2] S. P. Ó Ríordáin and J. B. Foy, 'The Excavation of Leacanabuaile Stone Fort', in the *Journal of the Cork Historical and Archaeological Society*, XLVI (1941), 87.

28   Cashel near Kilmalkedar, Co. Kerry

standard, although, like Grianan Aighligh, it was rather fancifully restored in the nineteenth century. The rampart, which is stepped on its inner face, has a gateway to the north-east. Foundations of several clochán, which are known to have existed as ruins early in the nineteenth century,[1] remain within the cashel. An interesting feature is the crescent-shaped annexe bounded by a much narrower wall which loops out from the main cashel and surrounds some two-thirds of it. A smaller, roughly square-shaped enclosure projects from this crescent to the north-east. There are no signs of dwelling houses within the annexe, which was, however, possibly used as additional living space as was the case in 'double-raths'. It may, alternatively, have been built as a cattle-enclosure when the number of clochán within the cashel

[1] Lord Dunraven, *J.R.S.A.I.* xxv (1895), 269.

29 Dún Conor, Inishmaan, Aran

became too great for there to be space enough for the herd to be kept there overnight. Oghil Fort, in Inishmore, is similar to Dún Conor, except that there the annexe is in the form of a circular enclosure concentric with the cashel and entirely surrounding it. In effect the result is a cashel with two walls having a large space between them.

The same arrangement of concentric walls is found at Cahercommaun, near Corrofin in Co. Clare (fig. 30), where, however, there are no less than three walls, widely spaced. The cashel was built on the edge of a limestone cliff descending to the Glencurraun valley, and although questions of defence undoubtedly governed the choice of site, this does mean that the structure has the deceptive appearance of a cliff-top fort, like Dún Aengusa on Inishmore. Cahercommaun was not military in purpose,

57

30   Cahercommaun, Co. Clare

but domestic. Excavations have shown that it may have been the house of a local chieftain, yet with farming activities predominant: a centre for a cattle-raising community of some thirty or more people.[1] The central cashel is 100 feet in diameter with walls 28 feet thick and 14 feet high, having two internal terraces but no remaining signs of steps to the top. The foundations of about a dozen very poorly constructed dry-stone houses were traced within the cashel, but no post-holes were found during the excavations of 1934, conducted by the Third Harvard Archaeological Expedition in Ireland. An iron door-hinge points to the use of wood for house building. The two outer encircling walls which are much narrower and more crudely built than the main wall of the cashel, also end at the very edge of the cliff. Irregular patch-work construction suggests that parts of them may have been restored in quite modern times to enable the enclosures to be used as cattle-pounds.[2] This was clearly

[1] H. O'Neill Hencken, *Cahercommaun: A Stone Fort in County Clare* (Dublin, 1938), p. 2.
[2] *Ibid.* p. 7.

their original purpose, too. There are several hut sites within them which must have been built for the ancient herdsmen. A paved path, with low flanking walls, gave access to the central enclosure by passing through the two outer areas. Two souterrains came to light within the cashel. Excavation demonstrated two short periods of occupation, both within the ninth century. The inhabitants cultivated grain and smelted iron on the spot, but they were essentially cattle-men. They used wooden vessels rather than pottery. The finds gave no clue to the reasons for abandoning the site: if the very large number of cashels in north Clare all have equally short periods of occupation, frequent desertions would seem to have been the rule.

In the Dingle peninsula in Co. Kerry, cashels and clochán are clustered together in the two early settlements or 'cities' of the Fahan group. Here Westropp counted 460 remains, including 414 clochán.[1] The district is also rich in conjoined clochán— the equivalent in stone of a conjoined rath. Some of the clochán were built as recently as the mid-nineteenth century, and although it is likely that the large majority are ancient, there is really no way of telling this without excavation. They vary from 4 feet to 22 feet in diameter, and are oval and D-shaped as well as round. But the most characteristic feature of all of them must have been the corbelled stone roofs which once gave the beehive appearance to the clochán. The panorama of Glanfahan (fig. 31) shows the site of the early settlement hugging the hillside as it descends to the sea. The line of an ancient road is marked by a wall which forms the highest limit of the modern field boundaries. Beyond it, on the now abandoned upper hillside, are faint traces of ancient fields. Between the site of the old road and the modern lie the remains of the early settlement. There is a stone cashel, 75 feet in diameter (Caher Murphy), enclosing a group of conjoined clochán and a souterrain. Nearby are many conjoined clochán, some with forecourts and most with souterrains. One very unusual cluster ('Caherfadaandoruis') has three conjoined chambers, connected from end to end by a straight passage 74 feet long.[2] The whole settlement appears to date from the early Christian period.[3]

Groups of stone cashels with surrounding fields and associated works, similar in type though less elaborate than the Fahan complex, must have been reasonably common elsewhere in the west of Ireland. Ancient fields visible near the stone cashels at Carrig Aille, Lough Gur, Co. Limerick, are possibly of late Iron Age date.[4] An agricultural community existed around Twomile Stone, on a limestone ridge in

---

[1] Westropp, 'Ancient Forts of Ireland', p. 681.
[2] For a description of the Glanfahan antiquities, see George V. Du Noyer, 'Of the remains of Ancient Stone-built Fortresses and Habitations occurring to the West of Dingle', in the *Archaeological Journal* (1858), p. 1. His diagrams of the remains, on pp. 14–18, are still useful.
[3] See T. J. Westropp, *Illustrated Guide to the Northern, Western, and Southern Islands, and Coast of Ireland* (Dublin, 1905), p. 131.
[4] Ó Ríordáin, *Antiquities of the Irish Countryside*, p. 13.

31 Early settlements at Glanfahan in the Dingle Peninsula, Co. Kerry

southern Donegal, at about the same time. Here there are stone cashels, hut-sites and contemporaneous field enclosures. The fields themselves were large and irregular in shape, bordered with stone-faced walls. On the side of the ridge were terraces suitable for crops, and grains of wheat have in fact been found in the one hut excavated on the site.[1] It is possible that in a complex habitation area like this the cashels were the dwellings of the freemen and the huts those of the unfree.[2] Many ancient fields still exist in Ireland, especially on higher ground or on the sides of hills where more recent agriculture has not ventured. Most of these fields are almost impossible to date, especially since in parts of the country (notably in the rocky western districts) the shape of Irish fields has changed very little from prehistoric to modern times. Where the field enclosures are associated with surviving cashels the chances for dating are improved—but sometimes only marginally, for stone cashels continued to be occupied by farmers until the seventeenth or eighteenth centuries. Estimates

[1] O. Davies, 'The Twomile Stone. A Prehistoric Community in County Donegal', in *J.R.S.A.I.* LXXII (1942), 98.

[2] Michael Duignan, 'Irish Agriculture in Early Historic Times', in *J.R.S.A.I.* LXXIV (1944), 124.

32 Cashels and early fields near Corrofin, Co. Clare

of the age of fields of this type must therefore await excavation of their associated cashels or raths. In cases where this has already occurred—as at Carrig Aille, Two-mile Stone, and Cruachan—a late Iron Age date has been established with reasonable certainty. Field boundaries of that period were built of large stone slabs, about 3 feet high, set in vertical positions and often supporting an earthen bank.[1] There are good examples of stone cashels with surrounding early fields on a limestone hillside some 5 miles to the north of Corrofin in Co. Clare (fig. 32). There date is unknown, but the remains are of the Early Christian type and lie in an area where cashels of that

[1] O. Davies, 'Ancient field-Systems and the date of formation of the peat', in *U.J.A.* II (1939), 61.

33 Remains of ancient fields near Brideswell, Co. Roscommon

period are very common.[1] The hill-slope is parcelled into irregular fields, all walled in stone. There are three main cashels, with the foundations of internal dwellings clearly visible, and a number of isolated hut sites. Two rectangular-shaped enclosures may be cattle-pounds. A larger and more complicated system of fields and cashel groups is located on the Mayo-Roscommon border 3 miles to the east of Ballyhaunis. Here the chaotic shapes of the ancient fields have been divided by large modern rectangular field boundaries superimposed upon the whole area. These modern fields must surely have been intended only for grazing—perhaps a nineteenth-cen-

[1] T. J. Westropp, 'Prehistoric Remains in Burren', in *J.R.S.A.I.* XLV (1915), 266.

34　Raths and associated fields near Brideswell, Co. Roscommon

tury 'clearance'—since the early stone field boundaries have very largely survived intact apart from occasional quarrying for building-stone.

Roscommon is especially rich in early field-systems. Five miles west of Brideswell is an area of ancient irregular field-plots, over-ridden by straight modern boundaries which re-divide the land into rectangular fields (fig. 33). There are faint traces of ploughing in the small enclosures: a sure sign that the fields were arable rather than pasture. The survival of this run-rig would strongly suggest that these fields, whatever their origin, remained in use possibly even as late as the nineteenth century. Many earthen raths sometimes with associated fields surrounding them, are also found west of Brideswell. A small part of this complex appears in fig. 34, which

35 Cropmarks of a rath and associated field-boundaries, near Rathangan, Co. Kildare

shows a large rath, with internal subdivisions, and a smaller rath. Both have earthen banks (probably with a stone core), and both are linked to early field-boundaries also built of earth and small stones. Modern field walls cut across the site, bisecting the smaller rath. Surviving traces of run-rig again suggest that this agriculture may be no older than medieval: only excavation of the raths could decide the date. Probably the fields and dwellings are of the Early Christian period, but retained in use to a much later date. But the site, whatever its precise age, affords a clear picture of a typical early agricultural community settled on comparatively fertile lands. Near Rathangan in Co. Kildare a chance photograph of a cropmark of a large rath also revealed associated fields (fig. 35). Only about a half of the site is visible, extending

64

over most of a sizeable modern field. The early field boundaries are of irregular looped and roughly rectangular shapes, radiating outwards from the rath like the petals of a flower. Some of them are over-ridden by much later field-boundaries, which have in turn disappeared, as amalgamation of small plots has yielded the larger modern fields.

Irish raths are almost identical, in both purpose and shape, with the Late Iron Age 'rounds' of Cornwall and Devon, and the 'rounds', too, had their field systems directly attached to them.[1] Early fields associated with raths are found to the south of the important Rathcroghan remains in Roscommon. The most obvious earthwork here is a large circular enclosure, 336 feet in diameter, with stone-faced walls, known as Relig na Ríogh (fig. 36). The name—the anglicised version is given on the first Ordnance Survey of 1838—suggests a royal burial place, and antiquarians for long supposed that such was its character.[2] The 1838 map marks as a grave a large stone within the earthwork. Excavations, however, have revealed no trace of burials,[3] and the earthwork is likely to have been a very large cattle-enclosure: perhaps it once protected the royal herds of the Connacht kings who dwelt at Rathcroghan. There are internal subdivisions which may have served to separate the cattle into different herds. (The scale of the enclosure is suggested in the photograph by a herd of cows actually grazing in and around it.) Small, roughly rectilinear fields abutt the enclosure, and just to the north the land is covered with early field boundaries[4] amongst which lie two raths. To the north-west, partly included within a large rectangle, marked by a modern stone wall, a complicated settlement is represented by hut-foundations, access-ways, and small fields. To the north of that again, there are larger ancient fields with very substantial stone-faced banks.[5] The whole area, including Relig na Ríogh and the two raths, appears to be enclosed by an extensive earthen embankment. Altogether it seems to have formed a considerable agricultural satellite of Rathcroghan—the royal farm, as it were. The small fields must have been for arable farming, and the larger ones for pasture. Large cattle-pounds, though unusual, are not actually rare. Their circular walls and internal subdivisions sometimes appear as cropmarks—a clear example near Manorcunningham in Co. Donegal is shown in fig. 37. In the stone areas of the west, and especially in the Burren country of Co. Clare, many more examples have survived than in the lowlands. This is partly, of course, because a larger number of cattle-pounds were required in the upland

---

[1] See Charles Thomas, 'The Character and Origins of Roman Dumnonia', in *CBA Research Report* **7** (London, 1966), p. 87

[2] See T. J. Westropp, 'The Ancient Forts of Ireland', p. 643.

[3] Evans, *Prehistoric and Early Christian Ireland*, p. 184.

[4] H. T. Knox, 'Ruins of Cruachan A I', in *J.R.S.A.I.* XLIV (1914), 28.

[5] See Sir Samuel Ferguson, in *P.R.I.A.* I (1879), ser. ii, 114.

36 Relig na Ríogh, near Rathcroghan, Co. Roscommon

pastures, but also because the levelling of sites by ploughing has been far more frequent in lowland districts.

Irish fields of the Iron Age were typically of irregular shape and scattered around the farmsteads. Attention should be drawn, however, to the cropmarks of field

37 Cropmarks of a cattle-enclosure near Manorcunningham, Co. Donegal

boundaries discovered near Lady's Island in Co. Wexford (fig. 38). Small and compact rectilinear fields can there be seen lying beneath the modern ones. In size and shape they are similar to the 'Celtic' fields of Wessex and the 'irregular checker-board of small rectilinear plots'[1] found associated with Iron Age settlements in the uplands of Cornwall and Devon, but they are very unlike any known early Irish systems. They do compare, on the other hand, with fields attributed to the pre-Roman Iron Age in Denmark. Fig. 39 shows cropmarks of ancient fields near Alslev on the west coast of the Jutland province of Ribe. The two patterns are so similar

[1] Thomas, 'Character and Origins of Roman Dumnonia', p. 94.

5-2

that some connection seems certain, and it is tempting to suggest that the Wexford fields were laid out by Viking settlers. Wexford, after all, as its name suggests, was an area where Viking settlements were concentrated. And it would certainly be a most important discovery should the fields be Norse in origin, Viking remains being very scant in Ireland since most of their settlements now lie beneath urban areas and their immediate hinterlands. But there must be reservations. The Danish fields of this type are usually thought to belong to the pre-Viking Iron Age,[1] and typical Viking fields are believed to have had long strips. Nothing is actually clearly established, however, and these small rectilinear fields *may* have been just as typical of the Viking era. It is also true that the most influential Viking influence in Ireland was Norwegian. The annalists describe the arrival of the 'dark foreigners'—usually identified with the Danes—in 851, by which time they had to contest areas for settlement with their predecessors. Yet southern Wexford like other places of easy access along the east coast is likely to have been among the first places they successfully intruded. It could also be that the connection between the Danish and the Wexford fields lay in a 'Celtic' source, originally foreign to both. On balance, the supposition that these Wexford fields are Viking has much to commend it.

The equivalent of the stone cashel groups of the west of Ireland are the rath clusters found in the fertile lands of the rest of the country. Ó Ríordáin believed that groups of raths were extremely rare,[2] and cited the example at Cush in Co. Limerick, as if almost unique. At Cush the southern group consists of six small conjoined earthen raths, each around 65 feet in diameter, some with one rampart and some with two. During the excavations of 1934–5, a rectangular enclosure attached to the cluster was found to contain five house sites.[3] Around these earthworks lie ancient fields, almost certainly contemporaneous with the raths, to which the boundary fences are in some places actually attached. Excavations showed that these fences were of simple construction—a very low bank and a shallow ditch. The modern field pattern is superimposed upon the ancient one. The date of the raths and their fields has been ascribed both to the Early Iron Age,[4] and to the Early Christian period.[5]

The results of aerial reconnaissance would seem to suggest that rath clusters were very much less rare than Ó Ríordáin and others have thought, however. Groups of small raths have been recorded as cropmarks in several places. Probably they were once quite common, and have now disappeared because their rather slight construction made them early victims of medieval and modern ploughing. The small fields

[1] Ole Klindt-Jensen, *Denmark before the Vikings* (London, 1957), p. 95.
[2] Ó Ríordáin, *Antiquities of the Irish Countryside*, p. 12.
[3] Ó Ríordáin, 'Excavations at Cush', in *P.R.I.A.* XLVC (1940), 117.
[4] *Ibid.* p. 176.
[5] Evans, *Prehistoric and Early Christian Ireland*, p. 143.

38 Cropmarks of fields near Lady's Island, Co. Wexford

associated with rath clusters suggest that the communities who lived in them were largely engaged in arable farming. Perhaps they were families of (unfree?) men who were too poor or insufficiently independent to own cattle, but who were yet able to dig small circular earthworks within which they could build their wattle and wicker-work huts. Groupings of these small raths would naturally occur: arable farmers, and poor ones at that, must have had to share the same plough and other agricultural equipment. It may well be profitable to ask whether it is possible to detect two

69

39 Cropmarks of fields near Alslev, Ribe, Denmark

distinct rural economies at work in the early period. Could the more typical isolated rath farmsteads have belonged to men of substance and their dependents, engaged primarily in pastoral farming, and could the small rath clusters have belonged to lesser men largely involved in arable farming? The rich farming land on which the latter settled has everywhere been intensively cultivated in medieval and modern times, so that surface remains of early rath clusters have vanished. However, crop-marks may still bring them to light. Sometimes, as at Ardfert in Co. Kerry, these

40 Cropmarks of a rath group, Ardfert, Co. Kerry

small raths lie some 50 yards apart (fig. 40) from one another in a group. One of the three seen in the plate actually survives at the junction of a system of modern fields: the other two, one circular and the other D-shaped, are seen as cropmarks. The edge of the D-shaped rath is attached to what seems to be a contemporaneous field-boundary. Another rath cluster, and a very large and intricate one, has been identified as a series of cropmarks in several fields 3 miles to the north of Castledermot, Co. Kildare. Fig. 41 shows a part of the complex now falling within two modern fields separated by a road. At least five individual small rath sites are visible, appearing on the top of a low ridge of gravel where conditions have especially favoured the development of cropmarks, although two of these overlap suggesting re-building at

41 Cropmarks of a rath group near Castledermot, Co. Kildare

some time and a generally complicated history. Further photographs have revealed similar small raths in the immediate area, and since only parts of the terrain are especially conducive to cropmark development other comparable raths may well remain undetected in these fields.

4

IRON AGE DEFENCES

IRISH HILL-FORTS APPEAR as large circular earthworks having banks and ditches that describe the contour of a hill near to its summit: the hill may be a fairly low eminence, a focal point in rich farming land. Typical examples are univallate, and enclose a large area, sometimes more than 20 acres. A few, which perhaps bear some relation to British hill-forts, may actually date from the Early Iron Age. The complex defence system on Cathedral Hill, Downpatrick in Co. Down, for example, has been tentatively considered to span most of the Early Iron Age.[1] Navan Fort, in Co. Armagh, has yielded some finds of the first century, but the earthwork may itself be some two centuries older. A few of the hill-forts surrounded the palaces of provincial kings: if these can really be identified with the heroic age of their literary associations they may well belong to the fourth century A.D. The large majority of ordinary hill-forts seem to have been built in the later Iron Age. Freestone Hill, Co. Kilkenny, proved on excavation to be fourth century in date.[2]

The greater hill-forts were frequently built around a hugely older cairn or Megalithic tomb, and to some extent this must have been unavoidable since almost all the favourable summits were already so crowned. The existence of the ancient burial place unquestionably added significance to the site and imparted quasi-sacred qualities to which the hill-fort builders showed ample deference. The coincidence within the same hill-fort, of a Megalithic tomb and a royal residence, may have caused the tomb to have come, after a short lapse of time, to be identified with that of the founder of the dynasty. The large hill-forts which contain an older tomb tend to have *internal* ditches—the ditch inside the enclosing rampart—and this feature has often been supposed to suggest some vaguely ritual significance—as it were to keep the sacred protection of the inhabitant of the ancient tomb, and prevent his wandering spirit from straying beyond the enclosure; just as an external ditch prevented the entry of wild beasts and hostile raiders. Unlike ordinary raths, the massive earthworks of hill-forts must have been primarily defensive. There is archaeological evidence that a strong timber palisade once surmounted the top of the rampart at Tara, and such a definite feature is unlikely to have been absent from other royal citadels; probably status required it.

[1] Evans, *Prehistoric and Early Christian Ireland*, p. 23. *Archaeological Survey, Co. Down*, pp. 98-9. *U.J.A.* XVII (1954), 95-102.
[2] G. Bersu, *Old Kilkenny Review*, IV (1951), 5.

42   Hill-Fort, Dún Aillinne, Co. Kildare

The hill-fort at Knockaulin, near Kilcullen in Co. Kildare (fig. 42), though a rather special site, may be taken as a typical example. It is distinctive as the royal seat of the Kings of Leinster: the Dún Aillinne of heroic literature. The circular walls enclose an area of 20 acres and follow a contour course round a hill 600 feet high. The huge earthen ramparts, now partly obscured by bushes, still rise to 15 feet, and the internal ditch is 6 feet deep. At the centre of the fort, and on the summit of the hill, is a despoiled stone cairn, probably of Bronze Age date but re-used in the Iron Age.[1] Its present height of only 2 or 3 feet is the result of piecemeal destruction

[1] Evans, *Prehistoric and Early Christian Ireland*, p. 137.

43 Excavations at Navan Fort, Co. Armagh

wrought by men plundering the stones for field walls. There are faint traces of two small circular rath-like earthworks within the huge enclosure. As at Tara, ancient road-ways approached the site from several directions. Without archaeological evidence there can be no certainty about the date of the fort, but it is probably, as a royal residence, quite an early example, and could therefore be ascribed to the last two centuries B.C. A similar, though smaller hill-fort, served as the ancient seat of the Kings of Ulster. This is Navan Fort (Emain Macha) in Co. Armagh. There the enclosing ramparts are much less formidable, and the area only 18 acres. As at Dún Aillinne, the ditch is inside the ramparts; and at the summit of the hill is a mound which was found, on excavation, to have a core of stone rubble and turf.[1] It was

[1] *Northern Ireland from the Air*, ed. R. Common (Belfast, 1964), p. 36.

probably a tomb-site. To the south-east of the mound, are the faint remains of a small rath largely obliterated by the plough.[1] According to the literature, the fort was built for royal occupation around 300 B.C., and this could be its date. It must have continued in use as a palace until the fourth century A.D., although of the wooden hall of the prince there is, of course, now no visible trace. Excavations, still in progress, have shown that the central mound was subdivided radially, with walls like the spokes of a wheel: fig. 43 shows the site and the excavations in the summer of 1967.

The most famous hill-fort in Ireland is Tara, Co. Meath (fig. 44), the seat of the Uí Néill kings. The place is well-documented and there is no doubt of the identification from early accounts—even though the most useful of them, the Dindshenchas and the Book of Leinster, were written long after the great days of Tara had come to an end. The hill-fort itself crowns a low ridge some 500 feet high. It is an univallate, oval-shaped enclosure, 950 feet by 800 feet, known at the Ráth na Ríogh (or Royal Enclosure), and attributed to King Cormac Mac Airt. If this is correct this would suggest its construction in the third century A.D. The present dismantled state of the defences offers no indication of their original strength; excavations, on the other hand, have shown that the internal ditch was cut in the rock to a depth of 11 feet below the existing surface.[2] On the inside of the ditch was a trench which was at one time planted with large timber stakes to form a palisade. Like so many less celebrated sites, the Tara fort was built around a much older burial cairn—now known as the 'Mound of the Hostages', and seen on the photograph as a small circular eminence at the farthest (northern) side within the Ráth na Ríogh. Excavations between 1955 and 1959 established a double use of the mound. Originally a passage-grave of around 2,000 B.C. or earlier, it was later re-used for multiple middle Bronze Age burials. The stone cairn was covered with a 3-foot layer of clay. Within the Ráth na Ríogh the most prominent features are two conjoined rath-like earthworks. The eastern structure or Forradh (Royal Seat) is a typical bivallate rath 115 feet in diameter. Despite first visual impressions the rath has a slightly raised interior, within which a rectangular house-site may be distinguished. The western structure (or Teach Cormac) has ramparts which adjoin those of the Forradh. Within the raised interior is a modern statue of St Patrick and a monumental stone to the dead of the 1798 rebellion who were buried here. The most curious feature is the deflection of the outer ditch to incorporate the 'Mound of the Cow'—a more ancient sacred place and perhaps a burial mound. Two other burial places, in the norhern area of the Ráth na Ríogh, known to early-nineteenth-century observers, have since vanished

---

[1] *Ancient Monuments of Northern Ireland in State Charge* (Belfast, 4th ed., 1962), pp. 65–7. *A preliminary Survey of Ancient Monuments in Northern Ireland* (Belfast, 1940), p. 65.
[2] S. P. Ó Ríordáin, *Tara. The Monuments on the Hill* (Dundalk, 1954), p. 13.

44 Tara, Co. Meath

beneath the plough.[1] Just beyond the hill-fort and to the west of the tree grown churchyard lies the 'Fort of the Synods'—seen on the photograph as a roughly circular area of much disturbed ground. The destruction of the site was carried out by a party of British Israelites, who dug it over in the late nineteenth century during a search for the Ark of the Covenant which they had supposed was lodged there.[2] An earlier nineteenth-century plan drawn by Petrie shows that it was originally a bivallate earthwork, 100 feet in diameter. Recent excavations suggest that it was

[1] R. A. S. Macalister, *Tara. A Pagan Sanctuary of Ancient Ireland* (London, 1931), p. 27.
[2] *Ibid*, p. 31.

heavily defended, with ditches cut deeply into the rock, and with a timber palisade. There were also indications of both burials and dwellings of the first three centuries A.D. The site has been traditionally associated with three early ecclesiastical synods. Further to the north is the long, low rectangular feature identified as the 'Banquet' or 'Assembly Hall'. According to the Dindshenchas it was a long house with twelve or fourteen doors. There are actually plans of the hall (though very stylised ones) in the Book of Leinster and the Yellow Book of Lecan. Originally a wooden building, the hall was 700 feet long. It has not yet been excavated. To the west, and disappearing among the trees of the steep hill slope, are three circular enclosures. To the south of the Ráth na Ríogh, and in the foreground of the photograph, is a large rath, 300 feet in diameter (the 'Fortress of King Laoghaire'): rampart and ditch are best preserved on the western side, but much of the perimeter has been levelled by agriculture.

The tops of hills were not the only natural features which the early inhabitants converted to defensive purpose. Around the coasts more than two hundred promontory forts have been identified in Ireland. Most examples, like the hill-forts, belong to the later Iron Age. Three excavated sites in Co. Cork mentioned by Ó Ríordáin were of that period. There were, in those examples, also signs that the promontory forts were constructed primarily as places of somewhat temporary refuge, rather than for permanent residence. Like the raths, promontory forts tended to be used until quite late historical times: the Dooneendermotmore fort, in Co. Cork, contained a seventeenth-century house.[1] Forts of this type were created, as at Lurigethan in Co. Antrim, by isolating a headland, or rocky projection into the sea, with a wall of earth or stone. Sometimes, as at Lambay Island, Co. Dublin, there were series of ditches as well. Inland examples, in mountain areas, are not common, but where they do occur (as at Caherconree, Co. Kerry), the defensive works are essentially similar to those of the coastal sites. Inland hill spurs, in such cases, were chosen to achieve advantages otherwise provided by a natural cliff defence. Dubh Cathair, an Aran promontory fort on Inishmore, shows the main features of the coastal sites with almost exaggerated simplicity (fig. 45). The top of a narrow finger of rock pointing into the sea has been defended by a huge dry-stone wall over 200 feet in length, 20 feet high, and 16 to 18 feet thick. This wall has three internal terraces and seven flights of steps—it is, therefore, in its characteristic structure, like the walls of the great stone cashels. Within the defended area are foundations of stone houses, probably of the clochán type. One end of the wall, and a gateway, which existed in the first half of the nineteenth century,[2] have since fallen into the sea. On the landward side of the wall is an *abattis* of broken stones—outward facing needles of rock

[1] Ó Ríordáin, *Antiquities of the Irish Countryside*, p. 18.
[2] Westropp, *Illustrated Guide to the Northern, Western, and Southern Islands, and Coast of Ireland*, p. 79.

45 Promontory Fort: Dubh Cathair, Inishmore, Aran

intended to impede invaders and deter a mounted attack. This style of defence, known as *cheveaux de frise*, was employed in other Iron Age sites; at Ballykinvarga in Co. Clare, for example. The date of Dubh Cathair is unknown, but it can surely be safely assigned, on the evidence of building style, to the first three or four centuries A.D. Excavation is not likely to be rewarding since the whole site is an exposed shelf of rock. A similar fort, Dún Beag, lies in the Dingle peninsula in Co. Kerry. There, the huge wall cuts off a triangular-shaped headland. Four external earthen walls (with a souterrain beneath) afforded additional protection. There was a single clochán within the fort. At Ballykinvarga the *cheveaux de frise* is almost 50 feet wide (fig. 46). The ruined cashel it encircles is 150 feet across, and with walls which still rise to 15 feet on the eastern side where the huge stone blocks are best preserved. There was a lintelled gateway to the SSE., which gives access to a walled passage through the *cheveaux de frise*.[1] Beside the internal walls of the cashel are a number of

[1] T. J. Westropp, 'Prehistoric Stone Forts of Northern Clare', in *J.R.S.A.I.* XXVII (1897), 123.

46   Cashel and *cheveaux de frise* at Ballykinvarga, Co. Clare

hut sites and subdividing walls—in 1897 Westropp drew a plan of them.[1] The date of this site, which has not been excavated, is unknown, but typologically it must belong to the later Iron Age. To the north-east, on a slight ridge, is a smaller and much less substantial circular stone enclosure, with a single subdivision suggesting a cattle-corral. The surrounding area is divided into plots by early field-boundaries, even though the terrain is one of sparse soils and rock outcrops with signs of ancient quarrying.

Strategically similar to the promontory forts were the cliff-top forts, although there are far fewer of them. The cliff-edge cashel at Cahercommaun, in Co. Clare (fig. 30) is a structure of this type, though excavation showed that it was not a fort at all, but the enclosed dwelling and surrounding cattle-pens of a local chieftain whose concern was farming, not warfare. Prominent defensive features are to be found at another site which is otherwise very similar in design: Dún Aengusa, an Aran fort (fig. 47).

[1] Westropp, 'Prehistoric Stone Forts', p. 122.

47 Cliff-top fort: Dún Aengusa, Inishmore, Aran

Situated on the edge of a 300 foot high limestone cliff are a remarkable series of crescent-shaped walls enclosing a total area of 11 acres. There were originally four of these walls, each of dry-stone construction; though the outer one, once 8 feet thick, survives only fragmentarily on the western side (the foreground of the photograph). Between this outer wall and the third defence, is a wide belt of broken stones—a *cheveaux de frise*. The three inner walls are each terraced. The innermost defence, marking off the cliff-side habitation area, is a wall 12 to 14 feet thick enclosing a space 130 feet across.[1] Buttresses were added to the wall during the restoration works of 1884. There is a lintelled gateway to the north. A square rock

[1] Several people standing on the top of the wall in the photograph give some impression of its scale.

platform on the cliff edge itself can hardly have marked the site of the internal dwellings; nor was the fort ever circular, and therefore owing its present appearance to coastal erosion.[1] Dwellings which probably lay beside the enclosure wall, as at Dubh Cathair, have now completely vanished, and as the area is composed of naked rock there is no chance of any archaeological evidence. The date of the fort is uncertain. Traditionally it is supposed to have been built by men fleeing from the east of Ireland who found their last refuge in the Aran Islands. But this is scarcely probable. A bronze ring of the fifth century (A.D.) found on the site[2] no doubt gives the best hint of the main occupation periods; stone implements also discovered here need not be of earlier date. There is evidence from excavated dwellings elsewhere that primitive stone devices continued in use alongside more sophisticated inventions into the Early Christian period.

Archaeological evidence for the dating of early forts and habitation sites is generally rather slight in Ireland, with one notable exception. The lake-dwellings, or crannógs, often provide ideal conditions for the preservation of objects in wood, leather and wickerwork, not to mention domestic débris. The lake-dwellings are essentially defended raths; they are farmsteads built upon islands. Some of these island sites were natural. O'Boyles Fort in Lough Doon, Co. Donegal (fig. 48), for example, is an orthodox dry-stone cashel built upon a rocky islet. It is impossible to suppose that the surrounding barren terrain could ever have supported anything beyond a minimal quantity of arable farming, and it seems to follow that the occupants of the cashel must have been primarily cattle-men. Most lake-dwellers, however, had to create *artificial* islands for their homes, and the name *crannóg* implies that they were made largely of wood. The fabric of the islands varied. Some were merely reinforced natural islands, made larger by artificial additions. Dr Oliver Davies has listed four leading methods of construction.[3] The earliest in date was the crannóg cairn: a pile of stones raised upon the lake floor, with the posts of the dwelling-house driven into it. He cites late Bronze Age examples of the type. But most crannógs are Iron Age or later. Packwerk types were made by laying down branches, sand, stone and other débris, pegging them together with timber piles without imparting any regular structure. These were mostly of late date—medieval. The most characteristic Iron Age crannógs were either log-platforms, or clay mounds enclosed by stakes and reinforced with layers of loose stones. In the former case a circle of timber stakes might be driven into the bed of the lake at some shallow point off-shore and secured with wickerwork. It was then filled with layers of rubble and logs ferried to the site— and sometimes a floating raft was first loaded until it sank into position to become the floor of the structure. Mixed examples may result from occasional reconstructions of

---

[1] See R. A. S. Macalister, *The Archaeology of Ireland* (London, 1949), p. 280, who discusses this exploded notion.   [2] Westropp, 'Prehistoric Stone Forts', p. 74.
[3] O. Davies, 'Contributions to the Study of Crannogs in Southern Ulster', in *U.J.A.* V (1942), 17.

48   Island cashel: O'Boyles Fort, Lough Doon, Co. Donegal

an individual crannóg during the periods of its occupation. Once the artificial island had been made, a palisade of wood, or even a stone kerb, was built around it, and sharpened timber stakes were sunk into the surrounding water as an additional defence—the lake-dwellers' equivalent of the *cheveaux de frise* of the stone forts.[1] The family house, of wood or stone, was built within the palisade. The small, low-roofed wooden 'huts', not unlike large dog-kennels, which have been found in several crannógs (Kilnamaddo, in Co. Monaghan, for example) have been regarded

[1] W. G. Wood-Martin, *The Lake Dwellings of Ireland* (Dublin, 1886), p. 36.

as only used for sleeping, not for habitation in a conventional sense.[1] More probably they were storage huts—especially necessary since it was not possible to build a souterrain beneath a crannóg.

The distribution of crannógs, of course, reflects the incidence of lakes in the Irish countryside, though they may be related to a level of water-table very different from that now prevailing. Most examples are found in the north and north-west of the central plain—especially in Leitrim, Cavan, Fermanagh and Monaghan—and in Down and Antrim. In those places there are many shallow lakes and clay soils. They were also the most heavily wooded areas in the Iron Age. This may account for the excessively defensive character of the crannógs. They were, after all, only the homes of isolated farming families. Abundant remains of bones and domestic articles show beyond doubt that crannógs were inhabited over long periods, even centuries, and were not temporary refuges in times of trouble. Finds of querns and agricultural implements in many sites show that the farming economy appears to have been arable rather than pastoral—as it must necessarily have been, in clearings made between the lake-shore and the forest edge. It is hardly possible to practice pastoral economy in a forest clearing. Crannógs, then, are the woodland equivalents of the raths. For raths lay in much more open country where advancing dangers were visible at a distance, and where defensive features, if they were necessary at all, need be only of the slightest. The elaborate defences of the crannógs, and the very choice of a lake site, were guards against the invisible perils, human and animal, which might emerge from cover of the forests. Attacks on crannógs were actually recorded in the sixteenth century.[2] One of the Ulster maps of Richard Bartlett, drawn between 1601 and 1603, records such an attack in progress (fig. 49).[3] The site is not specified, but is certainly Lough Roughan in Co. Tyrone, captured by Mountjoy in 1602. Bartlett's illustration shows a roughly square-shaped crannóg, with a timber and wickerwork palisade, and two dwelling-houses. Particularly interesting are the lake-side fields on the left of the picture, clearly planted with corn. They are enclosed within an earthen bank, and open only on the lakeside itself. The surrounding land is not wooded. Today the crannóg still exists, but covered with trees and shrubs.

Surviving crannógs can still be identified as small islands in shallow lakes, or sometimes on peninsula sites—when the water-table has fallen causing the original artificial island to become dry land.[4] Occasionally crannógs are found in boglands during turf-cutting: here the drainage of the lake in which the structure was built has been complete. The first Irish crannóg to be explored, at Lagore, near Dunshaughlin in Co. Meath, appeared as a mound in the bog; and so did the two famous sites at Ballinderry in Co. Westmeath. Some crannógs are undoubtedly of very early

---

[1] Wood-Martin, *The Lake Dwellings of Ireland*, p. 37.   [2] *Ibid.* p. 148.
[3] *Ulster and Other Irish Maps c. 1600*, ed. G. A. Hayes-McCoy (Dublin, 1964), p. 20.
[4] Wood-Martin, *Lake Dwellings of Ireland*, p. 200.

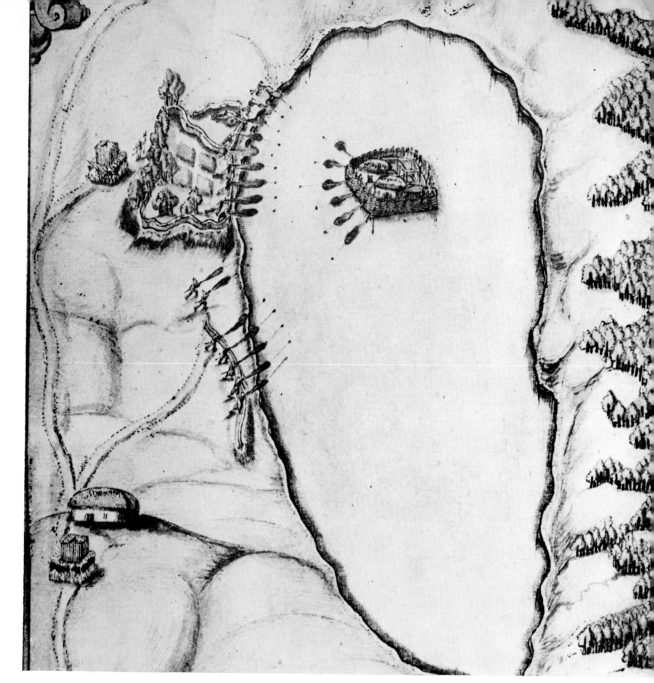

49 Attack on a crannóg. Drawing (*c.* 1601–3) by Richard Bartlett

date. Knocknalappa in Co. Clare, and Rathjordan in Co. Limerick, both seem to have been built in the Bronze Age.[1] The great majority of the known crannógs, however, including all the largest sites, belong to the Early Christian period. Lagore was built in the mid-seventh century and occupied until the tenth. Many of the splendid finds from this crannóg, giving a balanced picture of the domestic life of the time, were sold as curios early in the nineteenth century. The Ballinderry No. 1 crannóg was occupied from the late tenth century until the seventeenth century, though not, perhaps, continuously. It was built on a 20 foot square platform of logs,

[1] Ó Ríordáin, *Antiquities of the Irish Countryside*, p. 51.

50 Crannóg in Lough Enagh Eastern, Co. Londonderry

covered with layers of peat and brushwood weighted down with large flat stones. Timbers laid across the top provided the foundation of a horseshoe-shaped house. A wooden palisade, 85 feet in diameter, protected the island. A good deal of reconstruction occurred within the palisade, and twice the dwellings were rebuilt.[1] This crannóg was approached, as many were, by a causeway lined with guide-posts. At Lough Enagh, in Co. Londonderry (fig. 50), the crannóg (150 feet in diameter) was reached by a causeway which still exists. This site, partly natural and partly artificial, is also a very early example. Three occupation layers have yielded pottery and flint fragments from quite early Neolithic times to the later Iron Age.[2]

Many crannógs are today covered with trees and shrubs—which grow well in the

[1] *Ibid.* p. 48. [2] O. Davies, 'Trial Excavation at Lough Enagh', in *U.J.A.* IV (1941), 88.

51 Crannóg in the Clea Lakes, Co. Down

rich humus of these small artificial islands. The Clea Lakes, flooded low lying ground in between drumlins 2 miles north-east of Killyleagh, in Co. Down, provide a typical example (fig. 51). The round wooded island, some 200 yards from the shore of the eastern lake, is a crannóg. It was built on a submerged platform covered only by shallow water. The lake floor is of boulder clay. The site was partially excavated in 1956 and found to have been constructed in layers of rock chips, earth and midden débris. Large stones were probably used as a foundation, and an original stone enclosing wall has been largely rebuilt. Exact dating of the finds was not possible, but the period of occupation had undoubtedly been prolonged. Pottery, pins, beads, a quern and iron slag from the main levels, are typical of the Early Christian period.[1] No pottery, however, was found in the lowest and earliest level—just as pottery finds are rare in excavated cashels of the period. Explorations earlier this century in the East Lake area revealed 'souterrain' ware fragments and medieval pottery.[2]

[1] A. E. P. Collins and V. B. Proudfoot, 'A Trial Excavation in Clea Lakes Crannog, Co. Down', in *U.J.A.* XXII (1959), 94. [2] *An Archaeological Survey of Co. Down* (Belfast, 1966), p. 183.

Some curious defensive structures of late Iron Age date, about which commentary can at present only be tentative, are the earthen banks demarcating ancient territorial boundaries.[1] They are still discernible in many places throughout Ireland, but the most famous examples are associated with the defence of the Kingdom of Ulster: the Danes' Cast in Down and Armagh, the huge oval-shaped earthwork 10 miles to the north-west of Dundalk known as the Dorsey, and the Black Pig's Dyke. The Dorsey is too large (300 acres) to be a fort, and probably served as a vast cattle-enclosure, for temporary use when the border areas of south-eastern Ulster were threatened by raiders from the south.[2] The enclosure is linked to the defensive system of the Black Pig's Dyke (or Worm Ditch). This discontinuous linear earthwork runs from Bundoran in Co. Donegal to near Carlingford Lough—a distance of 130 miles. In many places it has been destroyed by agriculture: fig. 16, for example, shows the dyke crossing the countryside near Granard in Co. Longford. Here, the earthwork owes its survival to its incorporation in field-boundaries, curving down from the distant lakeshore to the foreground of the photograph. It can be seen dividing the fields, partly as a long hedgerow, and partly (noticeably to the right of the foreground rath) as an earthwork. Apparent inconsistencies in the defensive lines of the Black Pig's Dyke may reflect actual alterations to the southern boundary of the Ulidian territory; and perhaps those sectors of the frontier left undefended were—as with Offa's Dyke in England—originally heavily afforested. The date of the earthwork must be later than the second century, when the Romans built their frontier walls in north Britain, for these perhaps suggested this type of defence to the Irish; and it must be earlier than the mid-fifth century A.D., when the Northern Kingdom it was built to protect was destroyed.[3] In its most characteristic sequences, the dyke is a substantial linear rampart built of earth and with ditches on either side, each originally some 10 to 12 feet deep. In places there was a low bank on the outer side of each ditch.[4] At its base the rampart was about 30 feet wide and rising to a height of 20 feet from the bottom of the ditches.[5] Timber supports were incorporated in the bank to strengthen it. The dyke can scarcely have been adequate defence against systematic attack but would certainly have impeded raiders and made it impossible to move cattle.[6] In a society continually given over to cattle-raiding, the dyke may have proved a formidable deterrent: it was probably built across cattle-trails, and this may account for its discontinuous character. In addition to the main line of the dyke there are

[1] Ó Ríordáin, *Antiquities of the Irish Countryside*, p. 15; Macalister, *Archaeology of Ireland*, p. 287.

[2] Comparison may be made with the earthworks at Stanwick in Yorkshire, a stronghold of the Brigantes.

[3] O. Davies, 'Excavations on the Dorsey and the Black Pig's Dykes', in *U.J.A.* III (1940), 31.

[4] W. F. De Vismes Kane, 'The Black Pig's Dyke: The Ancient Boundary Fortification of Uladh', in *P.R.I.A.* XXVIIC (1908–9), 301.

[5] *Ibid.* p. 303. See also *P.R.I.A.* XXXIIIC (1916–17), 539, for Kane's re-assessment of some of his earlier conclusions.

[6] This compares with the Devil's Dyke in Cambridgeshire.

outlying linear earthworks to the south (near Dowra in Roscommon and Granard in Longford, for example), whose exact relation to the main system is obscure.[1] Perhaps the outliers were merely advance defences. Raths are frequently found scattered along the inside line of these earthworks. Perhaps they were the homes of men who watched the approaches to give early warning of impending raids. At least six raths were built alongside the Doon of Drumsna linear earthwork—a mile-long stretch south of Carrick-on-Shannon.

[1] Evans, *Prehistoric and Early Christian Ireland*, p. 140.

5

EARLY CHRISTIAN SITES

THE FIRST CHRISTIANS IN IRELAND—who may have lived in the south within an area roughly denoted by the present diocese of Ross[1]—have left no traces of their faith which can be discerned upon the landscape. The same can almost be said for their later contemporary, St Patrick. The Christianity which Patrick introduced to Ireland was, of course, episcopal and clerical, and reflected the organisation with which he had familiarised himself in Britain and Gaul. But there were immediate problems of assimilating this structure to Irish conditions. There were no Roman cities in Ireland which could be adjusted to accommodate the new ecclesiastical sees—for there had been no Roman settlement of the country. The large raths and cashels of the native Irish chiefs were scarcely an adequate substitute since they were used as dwellings, and the great hills of assembly were inappropriate since they were set aside by tradition for specifically legal and military purposes.[2] Sometimes, indeed, a converted lord seems to have handed over one of his raths to the church, but when this happened the site became devoted entirely to ecclesiastical use, the bishop and clergy moving in and the chief and his family either moving out or adopting an ascetic life, so that the marriage of civil and ecclesiastical centres, which occurred in the former provinces of the Roman Empire and imparted distinctive and uniform features to church government, was wholly absent in Ireland. The ecclesiastical centres, of which there must have been a large number in Patrician and immediately post-Patrician Ireland, were typically isolated rath settlements. These earliest sites were quite soon converted into, or occupied by, monastic communities.

Monasticism, once introduced, proved massively conducive to inherent Irish notions of overlordship and respect for kindred. Men and boys who had previously entered the learned class of pagan Celtic society by resorting in large numbers to the secular schools, now often went instead to the great monastic schools. By the end of the sixth century, many of the first ecclesiastical centres adopted monastic disciplines. This transformation was not quite so complete as was once believed, and as Dr. Kathleen Hughes has recently shown,[3] the ecclesiastical legislation of the seventh century seems to indicate that a non-monastic secular clergy, subordinate

---

[1] J. F. Kenny, *The Sources for the Early History of Ireland. An Introduction and Guide*, vol. I. *Ecclesiastical* (New York, 1929), 310.
[2] John Ryan, *Irish Monasticism, Origins and Early Development* (London, 1931), p. 88.
[3] Kathleen Hughes, *The Church in Early Irish Society* (London, 1966), p. 79.

to bishops rather than to abbots, continued to exist. It is still true, on the other hand, that by the seventh century the Irish Church had become characteristically monastic, with abbots administering ecclesiastical property as well as exercising general government within the Church.

During the sixth century the Patrician houses had been over-shadowed by a series of great monastic foundations whose inspiration may have come from Britain. Chief among these were Durrow and Derry, foundations of St Columcille; Bangor, founded by St Colman; Clonmacnois, founded by St Ciarán; Clonard, founded by St Finnian; and Clonfert by St Brendán. The new houses of the sixth century frequently had widely scattered churches within their jurisdiction, and, even more characteristically, were grouped together in *paruchia* or *familia*, through loyalty to a common founder or founding tradition. Durrow, Derry and Iona were linked in the person of St Columcille.[1]

The early poverty of the sixth-century foundations gave place, in the seventh and eighth centuries, to wealth and frequently to power, as gifts of land and property accumulated through the piety of the faithful and as monastic labour on the land produced its own rewards. During the eighth century monastic ambition precipitated in actual armed conflict between rival houses over disputed rights and lands, and with monastic armies dispatched, occasionally, to support the secular princes on the field. There were, towards the end of the century, signs of reform: a great ascetic revival, in a sort of dialectical negation, produced a large crop of hermits and some new ascetic communities. Their withdrawal from the world was to the lonely cell situated upon an island or by a lake-shore. Islands and lake-shores were also the scenes of less blessed events towards the close of the eighth century. In 795 the Norsemen raided Lambay Island off the east coast. During the 830s persistent attacks began, the long vessels sailing round the coasts and up the Irish rivers and lakes, penetrating deep into the countryside to pillage and destroy the wooden farms and churches. The monasteries, with their precious shrines and reliquaries and their sacred vessels of gold and silver, were the richest prizes. Many were sacked frequently. There must, on the other hand, be reservations when trying to assess the impact of the Vikings on Irish Christianity. Our picture of events comes exclusively from monastic records,[2] and these lack objectivity in certain particulars. It is true that the Annals list over 900 burnings and plunderings of churches and monasteries, but, as Dr Lucas has suggested, the pagan Norsemen were not the sole perpetrators of outrage. Many churches were burned in order to smoke out fugitives seeking sanctuary there, and many monasteries were plundered not for their sacred vessels, but because the local laity had deposited their goods within the monastic enclosures

1 An t-Athair Tómas Ó Fiaích, 'The Beginnings of Christianity', in *The Course of Irish History*, ed. by T. W. Moody and F. X. Martin (Cork, 1967), p. 67.
2 Dillon and Chadwick, *The Celtic Realms*, p. 129.

for safe-keeping.[1] The native Irish had themselves begun outrages against the monasteries long before the Vikings arrived and joined in.[2] The Viking raids, like the early Irish ones, therefore, were not motivated by sacrilege or by distinctly anti-Christian feeling. Sometimes a local Irish chief actually allied with a Norse leader to conduct a joint attack on a particular monastery which might house the goods or persons of an enemy *tuath*. There was another effect on the Church: alliances were made between individual monasteries and secular patrons to provide protection, and these, together with the decline of the eighth-century ascetic ideal, involved ecclesiastical interests progressively with temporal fortunes. The Church was still monastic in character, even after the conversion of those Vikings who had, from the middle of the ninth century, begun to settle in the country. And the Church's recovery, during the tenth century, with the final relaxation of external pressures, and in the eleventh century, after Brian Boru had contrived the creation of a coherent high-kingship, only tended to reveal the administrative inadequacies of its monastic structure. The converted Vikings were reluctant to place their own churches under the native abbots, and began to appeal to Christian authority overseas.[3] The result was the Irish reform movement which issued, at the Synod of Cashel in 1110, in a regular system of ecclesiastical government by archbishops and bishops. The ascendancy of the great monastic houses was then at an end. Their final collapse was initiated by the importation of systematic European monasticism through the British Isles: in 1142 the Cistercians founded Mellifont on a site not far distant from Buite's ancient community at Monasterboice. As it prospered and expanded, the older establishment waned and disappeared.

Before describing the traces which remain of these early monastic settlements, some brief summary should be made of their general appearance. Of the very first churches of the fifth century there are no remains at all. Built of wood—in a land still partially covered with forests—churches of the earliest type are described in later Irish writings. Churches were rectangular in shape, usually of modest proportions, but occasionally large, as the one in seventh-century Kildare seems to have been.[4] These buildings were situated within a circular enclosing wall made of earth and small stones, which might well be an ordinary rath and the former house of a rich farmer or chief. Now it is impossible to discern any trace of these first buildings, not simply because the wooden structures were replaced by later stone ones, but because everywhere the Patrician sites, in transforming themselves into monastic communi-

---

[1] A. T. Lucas, 'Irish-Norse Relations: Time for a Reappraisal', in *Journal of the Cork Historical and Archaeological Society*, LXXI (1966), 62–3.

[2] A. T. Lucas, 'The Plundering and Burning of Churches in Ireland, 7th to 16th Century', in *North Munster Studies* (1967), p. 174. But it should be noticed that Dr Lucas's compilation of statistics is based upon criteria which are in some large degree arbitrary.

[3] Máire and Liam de Paor, *Early Christian Ireland* (London, 1964), p. 172.

[4] *Patralogia Latina*, lxxii, col. 789, trans. Ludwig Bieler, *Ireland* (Dublin, 1963), p. 28.

ties during the sixth and seventh centuries, considerably expanded and covered the earlier Christian places with oratories and cells. Only the circular enclosing walls remained intact. It is, indeed, possible that some of the first settlements survived in another use altogether: the *Cillíni*, of which there are an especially large number in the south-west of Ireland, are probably very early church sites. They are large circular enclosures, with quite low surrounding walls of earth or stone, and usually with traces of early buildings in a demarcated sub-enclosure. Many have ogham stones, and all have served as burial places. Traditionally they have enclosed the remains of unbaptised children.[1]

The early monasteries, in their shape and general plan, must have been almost identical with the church centres: it was their size and internal discipline which distinguished them. The buildings were first of wood, and then—perhaps even as early as the seventh century—of stone and mortar. Stone construction became more general during the period of the Viking raids, when so many of the first structures had to be replaced after sackings and burnings: stone had the obvious advantage of being more durable. The tall stone belfry-towers were another response to the evil days. Most were built in the tenth century, and clearly had a secondary function as watch-towers. They are found exclusively on monastic sites, and some eighty survive, in varying degrees of ruination, to the present time. The first stone churches preserved something of the formalised design of the wooden buildings they replaced—as in the boat-shaped Gallarus Oratory in Kerry.[2] In many parts of the western sea-board of the country, where there were no trees, monasteries were constructed in stone from the beginning, and it is in surviving examples from those areas that the design of an early site can be seen most completely. The monastic cashel on Illauntannig Island, Co. Kerry (fig. 52), contains the substantial ruins of a dry-stone oratory, three clochán, three graves and a cross. The cashel walls of limestone are eighteen feet thick. The site is not quite intact, since about a third of the south side of the earliest enclosing wall has fallen into the sea through coast erosion. This has given the monastery the character of a promontory fort: but it was not one originally. When members of the Royal Society of Antiquaries visited the island in 1897 a small fragment of a second oratory was still in existence: this has since disappeared over the cliff. They also noticed 'the bones of its crowded cemetery projecting from the face of the bank'.[3] The more famous early cashel at Inishmurray Island, Co. Sligo, is in many respects similar to Illauntannig. At this site there are massive surrounding walls, 13 feet high and between 7 and 15 feet thick, within which there are a clochán, a small oratory—'St Molaise's House' and two other churches. There are internal enclosing walls. The monastery, which was frequently raided by

---

[1] Evans, *Prehistoric and Early Christian Ireland*, p. 33; Ó Ríordáin, *Antiquities of the Irish Countryside*, p. 22.
[2] de Paor, *Early Christian Ireland*, p. 57.　　　[3] *J.R.S.A.I.*, Proceedings, XXVII (1897), 291.

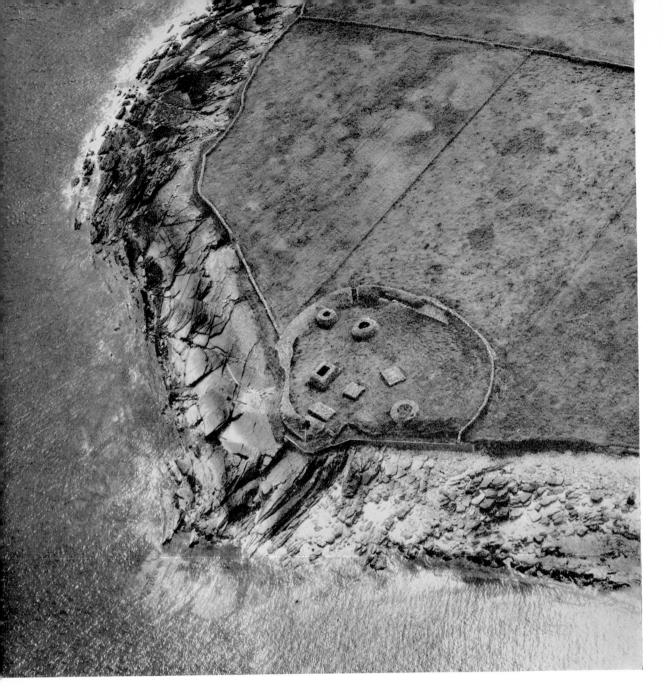

52 Monastic cashel, Illauntannig Island, Co. Kerry

Vikings, was abandoned in the ninth century. The remaining buildings are probably seventh- and eighth-century work, kept in reasonable order by the islanders, who used them for storage and cattle until their own quite recent desertion of the island.[1]

Those early communities who established themselves upon really desolate sites could not always surround themselves with circular walls like those of Illauntannig and Inishmurray. On the island rock of Great Skellig the early monastery had to

[1] Westropp, *Illustrated Guide to the Northern, Western, and Southern Islands, and Coast of Ireland*, p. 7.

53 Skellig Michael, Co. Kerry

cling where it could, and very inventive the monks were too (fig. 53). The origin of
Skellig Michael (Sceilg Mhichíl) is unknown, though it has been attributed to St
Finan (Fionán), and supposedly dedicated, like so many high places, to St Michael.

The monastery, despite its impregnable appearance, was successfully raided by the
Vikings in 823. It is not heard of after the middle of the eleventh century. Yet it
is the most perfectly preserved of ancient Irish monastic sites. The monks built their
cells within a series of enclosing terrace-walls on the steep eastern sides of the rock,
some 600 feet above the sea. There are six dry-stone clochán of corbelled work, a
Gallarus-type oratory, and a later church ('St Michael's Church'). At the higher end
of the shelf is a second, smaller oratory, and in the saddle between the two parts of the
island is an enclosure which may have been the cemetery.[1] In many places there are
walled-in ledges forming small artificial terraces of earth which were used for the
cultivation of herbs and vegetables.

The typical early monasteries, however, of which hundreds were established,

[1] Liam de Paor, 'A Survey of Sceilg Mhichíl', in *J.R.S.A.I.* LXXXV (1955), 174.

95

were always situated within circular enclosing walls or earthworks. Many of those founded in the older upland areas of settlement were simply built within the forts and raths presented to the local saints by grateful lords: the literature frequently mentions such gifts, and the practice seems to have continued until as late as the eleventh century. When a founder established himself in the lowland forests, or in the valleys, where there had only been sparse settlement previously, the enclosing walls must have been marked out on a completely undisturbed site. Professional rath-builders actually existed in fifth and sixth century Ireland, but it seems unlikely that the monks were either inclined, or could afford, to employ their services.[1] Sometimes the walls were surmounted by wooden stakes, but these were not intended as aids to defence: they were to keep cattle out and perhaps to provide additional privacy for the community. Monastic walls were only of deliberately defensive construction during the Viking period. In those places where land contour or rocky surface prohibited completely circular enclosures, as at Glendalough and Clonmacnois, the walls formed slightly irregular areas, such as a D-shape or a pear-shape. Where a pre-Christian site was occupied by a community of monks the earlier fortifying walls remained—as at Nendrum, where there were three concentric walls, or at Fenagh, where aerial photography has revealed double earthworks of quite intricate defensive design. Multivallate examples were presumably the gifts of very substantial chiefs—since multivallate raths were an indication of superior status.

Within a typical enclosure was a series of subdividing walls. Their function is not too clear. In many early monasteries the monastic clients lived inside, and since in the Church at Kildare the clergy and laity are known to have been separated by a dividing wall in the seventh century, it seems that this might well provide a general explanation. Inside the large enclosure of a typical community was a group of buildings: the church, a sacristy, and a walled cemetery. Nearby were the kitchen, which also served as a refectory, and a guest-house. Scattered around all these, yet still within the main enclosure, were the little cells of the monks—small round or rectangular huts. As a particular community developed, additional special huts had to be provided for scribes, metal-craftsmen, and so on. Instead of enlarging the size of the original founder's oratory when there were too many monks to worship in it, a second, and then a third church would be built within the enclosure. The sheer limits of the enclosing walls must ultimately have prescribed an end to this expansion—but only to expansion within the walls. Later writings describe huge communities with thousands of members, and although monkish imagination may well have tended to pious overstatement, the growth of monastic 'cities' around the original enclosures certainly suggest very substantial populations at the more celebrated

[1] Ryan, *Irish Monasticism*, pp. 245 ff.

96

foundations. As the monasteries became centres for metalworking and other crafts, specialist workers no doubt established themselves outside their walls; lay dependents and clients of the monasteries frequently built huts there too. In the seventh century students came from Britain and Gaul to attend the more famous monastic schools—these, also, would have required accommodation. In a society which had not built towns, these large monastic establishments must indeed have provided the only concentrations which looked at all like cities. Thus the later estimates of some 3,000 members of the celebrated monastic school of Clonard, Co. Meath, may well exaggerate the number of actual monks, and may even include daughter-houses in the estimate, but may not have exaggerated the total population drawn to the site of the monastery through its influence, and living in settlements thrown up around the original monastic enclosure. Aerial photography of the site today reveals the earthwork remains of a very extensive 'ecclesiastical city' (fig. 67). Beyond the walls of a typical community there also lay the fields, pastures, and farm-buildings belonging to the monks. The Church had deliberately sought to foster agricultural tillage to feed their more concentrated population in a land where the prevailing pastoral economy was redolent of pagan beliefs. The monasteries therefore promoted arable farming.[1]

The concentric enclosures at Nendrum, Co. Down (fig. 54), were found to be unnecessarily formidable by the monks who came to inhabit the site. Excavations have suggested that the pre-Christian cashel had no defensive value to the community, and that the monks filled in the space between the two inner walls to make a terrace.[2] Macalister believed that the site was originally a pagan sanctuary, and related this to a general conviction that most of the early monasteries were established where previously there had been pagan shrines.[3] Nendrum was excavated between 1922 and 1924, when the cashel walls were discovered. The community was founded around 445 by St Mochaoi (said to have been converted by St Patrick)[4] on an island in Strangford Lough. After being sacked and burned by the Vikings in 974 the monastery seems to have come to an end, and the church alone appears to have remained in use. The last documentary evidence of worship there is for 1450, and seventeenth-century sources refer only to ruins on the site. By 1844, when the monastery was rediscovered, the cashel walls had been buried, shrubs obscured the church foundations, and only the stump of the round tower—then imagined to be an obsolete lime-kiln—was visible. Today, after excavation, the site of the early monastery is seen to cover an area of six acres. The exposed foundations of the church are

---

[1] Evans, *Prehistoric and Early Christian Ireland*, p. 32.
[2] See H. C. Lawlor, *The Monastery of Saint Mochaoi of Nendrum* (Belfast, 1925).
[3] Macalister, *Archaeology of Ireland*, (foreword), p. vi.
[4] It has recently been suggested, however, that the monastery owed its inspiration to St Ninian and Candida Casa rather than to the Patrician tradition. See E. S. Towill, 'Saint Mochaoi and Nendrum', in *U.J.A.* XXVII (1964), 103.

54 Monastic site, Nendrum, Co. Down

in the central enclosure: they are of a twelfth century structure, presumably occupying the position of St Mochaoi's original oratory. The foundations of four circular monastic cells, of dry-stone construction, can be seen between the two inner concentric walls, on the western (right-hand) side. The round tower, by the church, must once have been some 50 feet high, and unquestionably dates from the period of the first Viking raids. Despite the strong traditional dating of the monastery from the fifth century, excavation of the site provided no evidence of habitation earlier than the start of the eighth century.

At Kilmacoo, near Kanturk in Co. Cork, a seventh-century monastic settlement

55 Monastic site, Lullymore, Co. Kildare

was made by St Mo-Chuda in the centre of a large trivallate hill ring-fort. The site today presents a pattern not essentially dissimilar from Nendrum, except that at Kilmacoo the enclosing walls are of earthen mounds, not dry-stone work. The central area contains the foundations of an early church. There are minor earthworks between the outer walls which perhaps indicate, as at Nendrum, the early construction of cells outside the innermost enclosure. Similar in appearance to Kilmacoo is Lullymore (Loiligheach Mhór), in Co. Kildare (fig. 55). In reality, however, the sites are rather different. Lullymore was said to have been founded in the late fifth century by St Erc. Many local legends associate the monastery with St Patrick, the

7-2

imprint of whose foot remains upon a slab of stone. The site is an 'island' $1\frac{1}{2}$ square miles in extent in the Bog of Allen. At the time of the foundation this remote place must have been surrounded by thick, wet forest. Its name can be translated as 'good grass for milch cows'. Tradition ascribes St Erc with the establishment of an important monastic school, which apparently long survived. In the sixteenth century a church was still standing within the present square enclosure at the centre of the site. Around this churchyard are the faint traces of a circular enclosing wall; and beyond that, is a clearly-defined bank and ditch of fairly irregular shape, now lined with small trees and bushes. These double walls initially suggest an earlier defensive site, as at Nendrum and Kilmacoo. At Lullymore there is no sign of a prior pagan use: there is, on the contrary, literary evidence which explains the outer wall. It was supposed to have been built in 722 by the sons and followers of King Hy Maine, to express their gratitude to the monastery for granting sanctuary after their defeat in the Battle of Allen.[1] The huge irregular enclosure made by these royal workers shows just how large the community of monks had become since the time when they were all able to dwell within the first small circular walled space.

The elaborate defensive walls of the Nendrum cashel were untypical of the early monasteries. Most had simple circular banks and ditches around them, usually about 200 feet in diameter, and made of earth and small stones. Hundreds were built and inhabited: only a few survive, since later monastic building on the earliest sites, or continuous use as a cemetery—as at Monasterboice and Clonmacnois—have buried all early features with later accumulation of remains. The earliest actual plan or diagram of a monastery is the highly stylised circular device on the last page of the eighth-century Book of Mulling, now in the Library of Trinity College, Dublin (fig. 56). It indicates two concentric circles representing the enclosing walls of the monastery of St Moling (Mo-Ling) by the River Barrow in Co. Carlow, probably founded in the seventh century, and long a place of pilgrimage. Crosses drawn within the inner ring of the device may suggest the extent of the monastic cells, and those on the outside of the circles have been thought to represent standing crosses.[2] It has also been argued that these crosses may denote the separate areas of sanctuary referred to in the canons of the *Synodus Hibernensis*.[3] At any rate, all traces of the rath have now disappeared, and the site of the ancient monastery of Teach Moling is largely obscured by a churchyard and by trees, although J. F. M. ffrench, at the end of the last century, believed that it would be possible to rediscover the site of the original enclosing walls by describing a circle, 175 feet in diameter, around the

---

[1] Mathew Devitt, 'The See Lands of Kildare', in *Journal of the Co. Kildare Archaeological Society*, IX (1918–21), 429.

[2] H. J. Lawlor, *Chapters on the Book of Mulling* (Edinburgh, 1897), p. 167.

[3] Hughes, *The Church in Early Irish Society*, p. 149. See also, Françoise Henry, *Irish Art in the Early Christian Period* (London, 1940), p. 101.

56 Circular device suggesting the enclosures of a monastery: from
the eighth-century Book of Mulling

existing ruins.[1] The monastic rath must originally have crowned the slight ridge
beside the river, and was probably a pagan fort—the *two* concentric walls indicated
in the Book of Mulling were surely defensive in origin—before the saint established

[1] J. F. M. ffrench, 'St. Mullins, Co. Carlow', in *J.R.S.A.I.* xxii (1892), 378.

his community there. The monastery was easily sacked by Vikings sailing up the navigable Barrow, and all the surviving remains—of cells, oratories, a large church, a high cross, and the stump of a round tower—date from a period considerably later than the Book of Mulling, and probably from the eleventh and twelfth centuries. The whole site has had a very disturbed history: in 1138 the monastery was burned down, and in 1323 it was plundered and burned by Edmund Butler, rector of Tullow. A town grew up around an Augustinian house established here in the thirteenth century. But of all this, aerial photography is unable to reveal much trace: the present use of the land is inimical to the appearance of cropmarks, and part of the site is wooded.

Kiltiernan, Co. Galway (fig. 57), is a good example of a typical early monastery. It is one among a cluster of similar sites in southern Galway: Ardrahan, Killeely, Kilcolgan, Teampull Geal, Caheradrineen, and Drumacoo. Nothing is known about the foundation of Kiltiernan. There was no medieval building on the site, nor has it been used for later burials. The date of the church ruins would appear to be late eighth or ninth century. The circular dry-stone wall is very large—enclosing an area of 4 acres—but is only 8 to 11 feet thick.[1] There is a gateway-entrance on the south-east side. Walls which subdivide this great enclosure produce some fifteen separate internal sectors. In a roughly square enclosed plot in the centre is a pre-Romanesque nave-and-chancel church. There are also, on other parts of the site, a souterrain, the foundations of three cells and half a dozen other fragments of buildings. Excavations in 1950 explored the central church area, which turned out to be a monastic cemetery. A few pieces of iron slag suggested that there was once an iron-works within the monastery; but no other finds were made which might help to date the site.[2] A very similar example is seen at Moyne Graveyard near Shrule in Co. Mayo (fig. 58). Here an early ruined single-chamber church with thirteenth century alterations stands at the centre of a large stone cashel wall which once defined a patrician foundation.[3] Today, the site lies at the margin of an improved agricultural area, and looks out over waste land. Both the inside of the enclosure itself and the fields beyond it were under hay when the photograph was taken. To the south side of the church lies a small graveyard: this is now unenclosed. Several memorials still remain, and burials have continued to the present day. Within the large enclosure the faint traces of subdividing walls are also visible. Similar in many features, both to Kiltiernan and to Shrule, is the ancient monastery on an island near the Longford shore of Lough Ree: Inchclearaun (Inis Chlothraun; Inis Cleraun). It is part of a complex of early houses, most of which are on the

---

[1] T. J. Westropp, 'Notes on Several Forts in Dunkellin and other parts of Southern Co. Galway', in *J.R.S.A.I.* XLIX (1919), 178.
[2] Michael Duignan, 'Early Monastic Site, Kiltiernan East Townland', in *J.R.S.A.I.* LXXXI (1951), 73.
[3] *Journal of Galway Archaeological and Historical Society*, VI, 104.

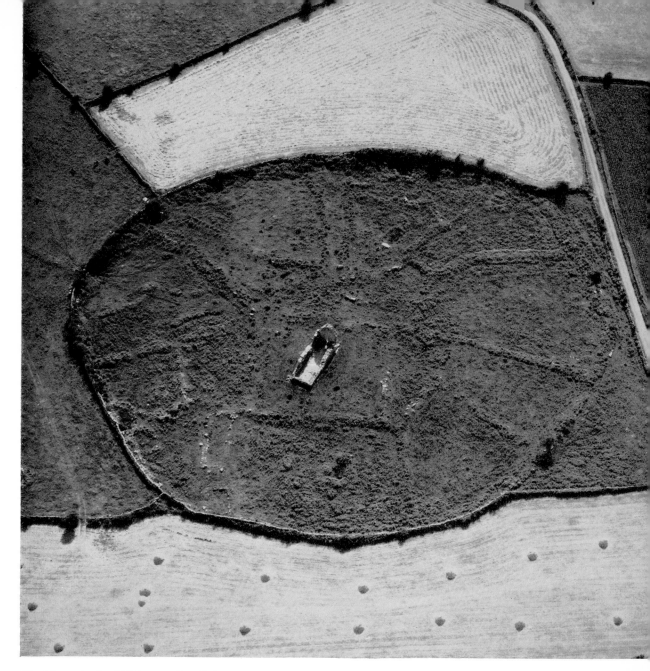

57 Monastic site, Kiltiernan, Co. Galway

Roscommon side of the lake—Hare Island, Inchmore, Inchbofin—all associated with Clonmacnois through St Ciarán. Inchclearaun was said to have been founded in the middle of the sixth century by St Diarmaid, the teacher of Ciarán, and is therefore in fact probably older than Clonmacnois.[1] The site is almost certainly that of a still older pagan shrine, and was also supposed to have been one of the royal residences of Queen Medb of Connacht. As at Kiltiernan, there are subdividing walls within a great circular enclosure of dry-stone-work and earth. Near

[1] F. J. Bigger, 'Inis Chlothraun (Inis Cleraun), Lough Ree: Its History and Antiquities', in *J.R.S.A.I.* XXX (1900), 69.

58   Monastic site, Moyne Graveyard near Shrule, Co. Mayo

to the centre are the oldest remains: two early churches, perhaps of the eighth century—Teampull Diarmada and the 'Church of the Dead'. There are also three later churches, of the twelfth and thirteenth centuries—Teampull Mór, the 'Women's Church', and Teampull Clogas. Nearby are some early gravestones, similar to those of Clonmacnois, and remains of conventual buildings, perhaps of the fifteenth century and not associated with the early monastic community at all. Another striking instance of a large monastic cashel is at Canons' Island in the River Shannon, Co. Clare (fig. 59). The original enclosing wall survives on the north and west side of a great compound, though now covered with trees and shrubs. To the

59 Early monastic cashel and later Augustinian house, Canons' Island, Co. Clare

south and east the line of the first cashel is maintained by a later and quite modest wall. The circle measures 320 feet in diameter, and encloses an area of 2 acres.[1] Within it, as at Inchclearaun, are later monastic buildings. A House of Augustinian canons was established here in the late twelfth century by King Donal Mór O Brien, but the existing structures date only from the mid-fifteenth century. Of the early monastery which must once have stood within the cashel walls there is now no trace.

[1] T. J. Westropp, 'Prehistoric Remains in Burren', in *J.R.S.A.I.* XLV (1915), 272 (footnote). There is a plan of the site on p. 271.

60   Monastic site, Rathcline Graveyard, Co. Longford

Another typical site (fig. 60) at Rathcline Graveyard, south of Lanesborough in Co. Longford, is also circular—though this fact is only clearly established by aerial photography. The single enclosing wall is now marked by hedges and ditches on one half of the perimeter, and by a slight bank across a grass field on the other. In this field the course of the buried cashel wall is marked by a moss-covered strip distinct from the normal grass surrounding it. The church itself—single-chamber Romanesque with later windows—is roofless and quite small; it measures 23 feet by 49 feet.

A hill-top site covered with earthworks is the most striking feature at Ardpatrick,

61 Monastic site, Ardpatrick, Co. Limerick

Co. Limerick (fig. 61). The early monastery, in a place where St Patrick is believed to have founded a church, was at one time extremely powerful and in a close relationship with Armagh. The present remains are of a large single-chamber church set in a rectangular churchyard, and of a 9 feet-high stump of a round tower just outside the graveyard wall.[1] The curving boundary on one side of the hill, though entirely modern in its present construction suggests a sector of the original huge enclosure of the

[1] H. S. Crawford, 'Ardpatrick, Co. Limerick', in *J.R.S.A.I.* xxxviii (1908), 76.

monastery. The sides of the hill, both within the enclosure and at lower points, are patterned with small early fields. Surviving scratch-marks on the surface, originally made by ploughing, indicate that these fields must have continued in use until comparatively recent times. But they are clearly of early origin—perhaps contemporary with the first few centuries of the monastery—and are an almost unique survival of the evidence of the ancient agricultural endeavours of the monks. An early entrenched roadway approaches the site.

The great enclosing walls of an early monastery were most likely to survive if they were constructed of stone, but aerial photography is especially valuable in detecting the location and size of monastic enclosures whose walls, whether of stone or earth, have been levelled and have disappeared. Earthen mounds were particularly liable to destruction, since they are especially common in the midland areas of Ireland where land passed most successfully into tillage. Aerial photography of the fifteenth-century church at Fenagh, Co. Leitrim (fig. 62), for example, which was known to exist on the site of an early monastery founded in the fifth or sixth century by St Caillín, has picked out the faint earthworks of the ancient settlement. The later church and graveyard is seen to occupy a position slightly removed from the centre of a circular enclosure with narrowly-spaced concentric walls. On almost directly opposite points of the perimeter are complicated right-angled turns in the outer wall—suggesting rather elaborate entrances to the monastic area. If the site was that of a still earlier pagan sanctuary, or the cashel of a converted lord, these extraordinary gateways would probably have had defensive purposes. The earthwork lies along the ancient boundary of the Northern Kingdom, and this may explain its heavily defended condition. Perhaps it was originally a boundary fort. Outside the enclosure a good deal of disturbed ground is visible, perhaps indicating considerable expansion and the settlement of monastic clients or craftsmen-apprentices. Kilcooly Abbey, in Tipperary, is a Cistercian house founded in 1182, though the existing remains date from the fifteenth century, set in the middle of the afforested Kilcooly Demesne. The original grant of land to the medieval monks by their patron, Donal Mór O Brien, which was rediscovered only in this century, shows that the Cistercian house was in fact built on an ancient monastic site.[1] An aerial photograph, taken in late evening sunshine, when low earthworks and disturbed ground not easily visible in ordinary light are sometimes detectable, has revealed the exact position of the early monastery (fig. 63). A circular rath-like enclosure, 200 feet across, with two ditches, is clearly discernible some short distance in front of the Cistercian ruins. It is unquestionably the site of the first monastery—perhaps of the early sixth century Daire Mór mentioned in the Annals.[2] Evident traces of disturbed land all round suggests that the original earthen enclosing walls were levelled by the

[1] M. Maloney, 'Kilcooly: Foundation and Restoration', in *J.R.S.A.I.* LXXIV (1944), 219.   [2] *Ibid.* p. 220.

62   Monastic site, Fenagh, Co. Leitrim

first Cistercians for agricultural purposes in the twelfth century. An air view of
Faughart, Co. Louth (fig. 64), shows, as a circular cropmark, the original large
bank and ditch enclosing the ancient monastery which once existed on the site.
The area is now bisected by a modern road. Supposedly the birthplace of St
Brigid, Faughart consists of a medieval ruined church (Teampull Āird), set in a
churchyard not far distant from an Anglo-Norman motte. In 1933 a small
shrine was built in the churchyard to contain a portion of St Brigid's head. The site
is traditionally associated with an early monastery, but it was always imagined that
this must have occupied roughly the position of the present enclosed churchyard.[1]
In fact the cropmark makes it clear that the existing enclosure is a medieval or later

[1] Henry Morris, 'Louthiana: Ancient and Modern', in *Co. Lough Archaeological Journal*, I (1905), No. 2,
19.

63 Kilcooly Abbey, Co. Tipperary, showing the circular earthwork of the early monastic site

one, and that the original circular enclosing ramparts of the ancient monastery were more extensive, defining an area almost three times larger. An access-way can be seen, also as a cropmark, joining the original monastery at a point near the Norman motte—and this presumably indicates the position of the gateway. Souterrains are known between the churchyard and the motte and these fall within the monastic area as now defined.

Many of the isolated single-chamber churches—of which there are so many in Ireland—in fact mark the sites of early monasteries. Aerial photography can sometimes pick out the faint traces of the characteristic circular enclosing walls, though

64 Faughart, Co. Louth, showing the original enclosure of the early monastery as a cropmark

these may lie beneath modern fields, hedges and roads. Where such an enclosure is plainly too large to have contained a simple graveyard (and graveyards were small in a country with modest units of population), it is a sure sign that the single church is a successor to an earlier oratory and is all that remains to indicate the site of an early monastic settlement. In this way, the present aerial survey of Ireland has added quite a few early monasteries to existing lists. Two examples will illustrate the point. At Tarramud, in the area of southern Co. Galway where many monastic settlements were concentrated, yet a new one appeared from a chance photograph of the small ruined church (fig. 65). Viewed from the air, the church itself is seen to be at the

III

65 Cropmarks of an early monastic enclosure, Tarramud, Co. Galway

centre of a huge circular enclosure. The single-chamber church is 19 feet by 40 feet, of modified Romanesque type. Part of the enclosure still exists as a bank and ditch, but most of the early monastic wall has been greatly reduced by ploughing in four other fields. A modern road, and field-boundaries, divide the site. And near Liscarroll, in Co. Cork, a small single-chamber church ruin (24 by 37 feet) and adjacent walled graveyard are also seen, from the air, to be situated in the middle of a large circular enclosure (fig. 66). The site is divided by a hedge, on the far side of which the line of the enclosing bank can be picked out as a low earthwork, the crop being discoloured on that line, and on the near side it appears only as a faint shadow.

Perhaps the most important early monastic discoveries made by aerial photography, however, will prove to be on the site of Clonard (Clúain-Iráird), Co. Meath (fig. 67), of which the de Paors have recently observed, 'no faintest relic of church or cell is now to be seen.'[1] The actual remains of church or cell are still absent, but the

[1] de Paor, *Early Christian Ireland*, p. 52.

66 Cropmarks of an early monastic enclosure, Granard Graveyard near Liscarroll, Co. Cork

general impression of the whole site can now be plotted by photography. The monastery at Clonard, on the banks of the Boyne, is dedicated to St Finnian, who died in 549. This saint, who had studied in Wales, established settlements in several places in Ireland until he was led to Clonard by an angel. There he built a church and cell of clay: the nucleus of what then became, for a time, the most famous and perhaps the most sizeable of all the ancient Irish monasteries. Students came from all parts of Ireland, and from abroad, to study in the great monastic school; the 'twelve disciples' of Finnian spread his influence and discipline throughout the country. The growing prestige of the monastery was reflected in donations of land,

67   Monastic site, Clonard, Co. Meath

and in the tenth century it reached the height of its prosperity. It was sacked by the Vikings in the ninth and tenth centuries, but recovered, and declined after 1206 when the Norman Bishop de Rochfort moved the see of Meath from Clonard to Trim. Medieval writers refer to the 3,000 inhabitants of the monastery, and aerial photography can show that this may well have been near to the truth. The site of the original enclosure is still suggested by the circle of trees, banks and ditches within which the existing Protestant church and farm buildings are situated. There are faint traces of a large outer encircling ditch, of slightly irregular shape, round this nucleus. The rest of the site is incredibly extensive, and consists of innumerable access-ways, square enclosures and of disturbed ground, perhaps marking the site of huts. The river itself once clearly ran, at this point, through a large 'ecclesiastical city'. The students, clients, and craftsmen of Clonard must have covered the ground with hundreds of straw-and-wattle dwellings and workshops. All have vanished, but the scars on the ground have remained, visible from the air in late evening sunlight.

Similarly at Drumacoo, Co. Galway (fig. 68), though on a much reduced scale,

68 Monastic site, Drumacoo, Co. Galway

disturbed land contiguous to the monastery can be seen from the air. On this site, the original enclosing walls of the ancient community founded by St Sarnat (or Sorney) in the sixth century have completely disappeared, apparently without trace. The ruined church is of eleventh-century construction, with thirteenth-century additions, enclosed within a rectangular space superimposed upon the original site of the early monastery. Nearby is St Sorney's well, in a small enclosure by itself. Beneath these ruins, and showing through the rough grass hillocks within the modern field enclosures, can be seen the small square and oblong traces of the first ecclesiastical settlement, with rounded depressions and stains in the soil suggesting

8-2

the foundations of cells or huts; with access-ways and perhaps garden-plots. None of these are discernible upon the ground.

Extensive earthworks, clearly seen upon the surface, are one of the principal features of the monastic site on Holy Island (Inis Cealtra), Lough Derg, Co. Clare. The island originally contained a pagan sanctuary, and then an early community of Christians, before St Cáimín established his monastery there around 640. Very little is known about its early history until the ninth century, and most of the remains date from after that time.[1] The whole area was subject to persistent Viking raids, and owed its later survival largely to the royal patronage of Brian Boru. During the later middle ages it appears to have become an ordinary parish, with St Mary's Church as the continuing place of worship. All the older churches—none of which are likely to date from before the eleventh century, however—were largely dismantled during the Reformation period. Only St Mary's appears to have remained intact, and was even enlarged late in the sixteenth century. During the following century the island was a refuge for Catholics, and some repairs to the ruins were undertaken early in the eighteenth century. In 1875 the local Board of Poor Law Guardians enclosed the cemetery, and in 1879 the Board of Works undertook restoration work on the church ruins and on the 75 foot high round tower. The earthworks cover the entire site.[2] Most pronounced is a D-shaped enclosure to the west of the round tower and St Cáimín's Church, within which is the square foundation of St Michael's Church and two trees. It was, perhaps, a burial ground. Some of the other banks and ditches define large irregular areas with straight sides, which must have been fields; others seem to have been access-ways between the monastic buildings. The clear definition of the earthworks makes it seem certain that the old monastic fields and paths must still have been used during the later middle ages, and perhaps even up to the eighteenth century, by successive inhabitants of the island; but that they were first drawn out by the earlier monks cannot be doubted, for they all relate closely to the locations of the monastic buildings.

It is impossible not to compare Holy Island with Devenish, Co. Fermanagh, which is also situated on a lake island. Devenish, in Lower Lough Erne, was founded in the sixth century by St Molaise (Mo-Laisse), one of the disciples of Finnian of Clonard. Though there are traces of earthworks on the site they are very much less obvious than those of Holy Island, and have survived too imperfectly to suggest a coherent pattern. According to McKenna, the original monastery lay to the west of the existing ruins of St Mary's Abbey,[3] and can still be discerned from the rounded earthen bank near the path which leads to the landing-place. This, he believed, was

---

[1] R. A. S. Macalister, 'The History and Antiquities of Inis Cealtra', in *P.R.I.A.* XXXIII C (1917), 93.
[2] See Macalister's line drawing of them, *ibid.* p. 174.
[3] J. E. McKenna, *Devenish: Its History, Antiquities and Traditions* (Dublin, second ed. 1931), p. 18.

all that remained of a large rath within which St Molaise settled his community. Aerial photography has not so far been able to establish the existence of this rath. Of the visible remains, St Molaise's House is the oldest—perhaps originally a late sixth century oratory, subsequently re-built in the Romanesque style. It was almost complete as recently as the eighteenth century, and engravings of that period show that it has a high-pitched stone roof. Its demolition, like that of other buildings on the island, was to provide building materials for the eighteenth-century expansion of housing in Enniskillen.[1] The round tower, built in the tenth century and restored in 1835 and 1896, is 81 feet high. Teampull Mór was Romanesque in style, probably late eleventh or twelfth century in date,[2] and was considerably damaged by a storm in 1780. It served as the parish church of Devenish, and is surrounded by an enclosed churchyard. The ruins of St Mary's Abbey, an Augustinian foundation, are gothic and of fifteenth-century date. The building was already ruined by the start of the seventeenth century, and early in the nineteenth was further dismantled when the site became a farmyard. The square tower, and fragments of the conventional buildings, are all that remain.

Some of the most famous early monastic sites are the least rewarding to the aerial photographer. At Armagh, however, where St Patrick established his principal church, the later streets of the primatial city preserve the plan of the original monastic enclosure (fig. 69). Probably the hill-top chosen by Patrick was already crowned with a hill-fort or a large rath, but even if it was not, then a large circular enclosure, following the contour of the hill, must have been built either by the saint or by Bishop Cormac. Subsequent building outside the walls respected the first arrangement of the hill-top. Today the cathedral stands at the centre of an eighteenth-century town plan which has—as the vertical photograph of the city shows particularly clearly—retained the original circular shape of the monastic enclosure. But some other famous sites have no remaining signs of their earliest buildings and walls. Kilmacduagh, Monasterboice, Clonmacnois and Glendalough have all been largely obscured as a result of continuous use for burials, and the land around them has been extensively re-employed for agricultural purposes. The ruins which have survived, neatly contained within modern enclosing walls, are usually of the eleventh century or later. At Kilmacduagh, Co. Galway, the scattered ruins, of cathedral and churches, date variously between the tenth and the seventeenth centuries—but there is no sign of the earliest monastic area, settled by St Colman MacDuach in the seventh century. The cathedral continued in use for worship until 1656, and during the eighteenth century many of the buildings, as at Devenish, were still almost complete.[3] The

---

[1] Lady Dorothy Lowry-Corry, 'St. Molaise's House at Devenish', in *J.R.S.A.I.* LXVI (1936), 270.
[2] Chart (ed.), *A Preliminary Survey of the Ancient Monuments of Northern Ireland*, p. 161.
[3] J. Fahey, 'Kilmacduagh and its Ecclesiastical Monuments', in *J.R.S.A.I.* XXXIV (1904), 220.

69   The city of Armagh: vertical photograph, scale 1:2400

round tower, 111 feet high and now leaning slightly, was built on the site of the early monks' graveyard.[1] At Monasterboice, Co. Louth, no trace of the original sixth century monastic enclosure of St Buite (Buíthe), or of the nearby convent of women which he also established, is now to be seen. The famous burial ground, with its high crosses, continued in use for centuries and is now surrounded by a modern wall. The round tower, 100 feet high, was burned in 1097, probably only some fifty years after its first construction. Of the church remains, one to the south is a nave-and-chancel building of perhaps the ninth century: the other is thirteenth century. Due to

[1] R. Cochrane, 'Some notes on the Round Tower etc. of Kilmacduagh', in *J.R.S.A.I.* XXXIV (1904), 234.

70   Clonmacnois, Co. Offaly

continual use as a cemetery the ground level has risen over the centuries; interments
have buried the site of the original monastery several feet below the present surface.[1]
The surrounding land has been consistently subject to heavy ploughing over a long
period, and this has destroyed any earthworks which may once have existed.

   There is, similarly, no trace of the first great monastery of St Ciarán at Clonmacnois (Clusin moccu Nóis), Co. Offaly (fig. 70). This was one of the most important early schools, founded on the edge of the River Shannon by Ciarán in 544, who
died of plague shortly afterwards. The community prospered under the royal

[1] See R. A. S. Macalister, *Monasterboice* (Dundalk, 1946).

patronage of the great Uí Néill families, and was linked with Saigher and Glendalough.[1] Sustained royal support no doubt explains the survival of the monastery in the
face of extraordinary adverse conditions: it was burned down thirteen times between
722 and 1205, sacked eight times by Viking raiders who had sailed up the Shannon,
attacked twenty-seven times by native Irishmen in various feuds and disputes
between 832 and 1163, and six times by Anglo-Normans between 1178 and 1204.
The buildings were finally dismantled by English soldiers in 1552. Despite these
desperate circumstances, the continuing resort of monastic clients, students, craftsmen and soldiers led to the accumulation of a very considerable ecclesiastical 'city'
at Clonmacnois, like that at Clonard, and some indication of its extent can be judged
from a reference to a fire of 1179 in which over 100 houses were destroyed. Of all
these ramifications of the early monastery few signs remain. At Clonmacnois today
a modern wall surrounds the famous churchyard, with 500 early grave-stones of
eighth to twelfth century date, the two twelfth-century round towers, and nine
churches. To the west is a motte crowned with the remains of what is probably the
thirteenth-century castle of the English Justiciar, John Gray. Ciarán's first wooden
cells and circular mounded enclosure presumably lay beneath the present churchyard; the ecclesiastical 'city', beneath the modern fields. Glendalough, Co. Wicklow,
was plundered and burned on a scale almost comparable with Clonmacnois.[2] In a
narrow valley in the Wicklow mountains, St Kevin (Ceomghan) founded his
monastery in the sixth century. Surviving remains point to the lake-side at the upper
end of the valley as the scene of the first settlement: there are the remains of a
clochán, a small oratory, and some artificial terraces—perhaps of the eighth century.
In its remoteness—it is accessible only by water—the first settlement was comparable even with Skellig Michael as a refuge from the world. A later monastic nucleus
was established lower in the valley in the tenth century: a round tower, the ruins of
an irregularly-shaped enclosing wall, and a group of twelfth-century church buildings now mark the site. A graveyard covers some of the area. As at Clonard and
Clonmacnois, the monastery of St Kevin at Glendalough seems to have attracted
a considerable dependent population,[3] but of the 'city' which became attached to
the community there is now no trace at all. Trees, burials, and—in so steep a valley—
probably floods, have both covered and eroded the original site.

In 1169 the Normans came to Ireland, and within a century something like three-
quarters of the country had been subjugated by them. Large pockets of bog, forest,
and upland remained outside their sphere, and in these places many of the old Celtic
patterns of living continued. Elsewhere the Normans brought peace and new

[1] Ryan, *Irish Monasticism*, p. 326.
[2] H. G. Leask, *Glendalough*, Official (National Monuments) Guide, p. 7.
[3] de Paor, *Early Christian Ireland*, p. 57.

measures of economic sophistication. The Irish among whom they settled combined some elements of the new order with some of the old, but the face of the countryside began to change. New towns grew up, to rival the Viking foundations at Dublin, Wicklow, Wexford, Waterford and Cork. A money economy spread outside the Scandinavian areas to which it had hitherto been confined. Raths and cashels continued to be lived in by the native population, and some new ones were built; but the motte-and-bailey fortresses of the conquerors replaced the multivallate raths of the dispossessed Celtic petty kings as the centres of influence. The Norman settlers built themselves strong stone houses, set within square bawns. The great Cistercian monasteries continued the ancient pastoral economy of Ireland, but in the east of the country especially, the Normans introduced more mixed farming with systems of large fields. As well as the Cistercians, the Benedictines and Augustinians moved across the Irish Sea, and the old monastic sites were progressively abandoned as they were superseded by the new orders. In the thirteenth century the friars came as well. The Normans settled in insufficient numbers to achieve an advanced destruction of the stubborn materials of Celtic society, and after a time they were themselves partially absorbed. But only partially: too much had by then changed for any really successful re-emergence of the old order. Along the coasts and in the plains, in the west as well as in the east, the face of the Irish countryside had been overlaid with the fields and dwellings of a new civilisation. The Celtic Iron Age was in radical decline.

SELECT BIBLIOGRAPHY

GENERAL WORKS

Ancient Monuments of Northern Ireland in State Charge, Belfast, 1928.

An Archaeological Survey of Co. Down, Belfast, 1966.

Chart, D. A. (ed.). *A Preliminary Survey of the Ancient Monuments of Northern Ireland*, Belfast, 1940.

Common, R. (ed.). *Northern Ireland from the Air*, Belfast, 1964.

de Paor, Máire and Liam. *Early Christian Ireland*, London, 1964.

Dillon, Myles, and Chadwick, Nora K. *The Celtic Realms*, London, 1967.

Evans, Estyn. *Prehistoric and Early Christian Ireland. A Guide*, London, 1966.

Henry, Françoise. *Irish Art in the Early Christian Period*, London, 1940.

Hughes, Kathleen. *The Church in Early Irish Society*, London, 1966.

Jackson, Kenneth. *The Oldest Irish Tradition: A Window on the Iron Age* (The Rede Lecture, 1964), Cambridge, 1964.

Macalister, R. A. S. *The Archaeology of Ireland*, London, 1949.

MacNeill, Máire. *The Festival of Lughanasa. A Study of the Survival of the Celtic Festival of the Beginning of Harvest*, Oxford, 1962.

Movius, H. L. *The Irish Stone Age*, Cambridge, 1942.

National Monuments of Ireland, Dublin, 1964.

Ó Ríordáin, S. P. *Antiquities of the Irish Countryside*, London, 1964 ed.

Raftery, Joseph, 'Air Photography and Archaeology', in *J.R.S.A.I.* LXXIV (1944), 119.
  Prehistoric Ireland, London, 1951.
  (ed.). *The Celts* (The Thomas Davis Lectures, 1960), Cork, 1967 ed.

Westropp, T. J. *Illustrated Guide to the Northern, Western, and Southern Islands, and Coast of Ireland*, Dublin, 1905.

Wood-Martin, W. G. *Traces of the Elder Faiths of Ireland*, London, 1902.

CHAPTER 2

Borlase, W. C. *The Dolmens of Ireland*, London, 1897.

Collins, A. E. P. 'Excavations in the Sandhills at Dundrum, 1950–51', in *U.J.A.* XV (1952).
  'Excavations at Giant's Ring, Co. Down', in *U.J.A.* XX (1957).

Daniel, Glyn E. 'The Dual Nature of the Megalithic Colonization of Prehistoric Europe', in *P.P.S.* VII (1941).

de Valera, R., and S. Ó Nualláin. *Survey of the Megalithic Tombs of Ireland*, vol. I, *Clare*, Dublin, 1961.

Eogan, George. 'The Knowth Excavations', in *Antiquity*, XLI (1967).
  'A New Passage-Grave in Co. Meath', in *Antiquity*, XXXVII (1963).

Jope, E. M. 'Porcellanite Axes from Factories in North-east Ireland: Tievebulliagh and Rathlin', in *U.J.A.* XV (1952).

Macalister, R. A. S., Armstrong, E. C. R., and Praeger, R. Ll. 'Report on the Exploration of Bronze-Age Carns on Carrowkeel Mountain', in *P.R.I.A.* XXXI C (1912).

O'Kelly, Claire. *Newgrange*, Wexford, 1967.

Ó Ríordáin, S. P. 'Lough Gur Excavations', in *J.R.S.A.I.* LXXVII (1947).
  'Prehistory in Ireland, 1937–1946', in *P.P.S.* XIII (1947).
  'Unrecorded Earthwork near Newgrange', in *J.R.S.A.I.* LXXXIV (1954).
  and Daniel, Glyn E. *Newgrange*, London, 1964.

Powell, T. G. E. 'The Passage-Graves of Ireland', in *P.P.S.* IV (1938).

CHAPTER 3

Bernard, Walter. 'Exploration and Restoration of the Ruin of the Grianan of Ailaech', in *P.R.I.A.* I (1879).

Bersu, Gerhard. 'The Rath in Townland Lissue, Co. Antrim. Report on Excavations in 1946', in *U.J.A* x (1947).

Collins, A. E. P. 'Excavations at Dressograth Rath, Co. Armagh', in *U.J.A.* XIX (1966).

Davies, Oliver. 'Ancient field-systems and the date of the formation of the peat', in *U.J.A.* II (1939).
'The Twomile Stone. A Prehistoric Community in Co. Donegal', in *J.R.S.A.I.* LXXII (1942).
'Types of Rath in Southern Ulster', in *U.J.A.* x (1947).

de Paor, Liam, and Ó h-Eochaidhe, M. P. 'Unusual Group of Earthworks at Slieve Breagh, Co. Meath', in *J.R.S.A.I.* LXXXVI (1956).

Du Noyer, G. V. 'Of the remains of Ancient Stone-Built Fortresses and Habitations occurring to the West of Dingle', in the *Archaeological Journal*, 1858.

Duignan, Michael. 'Irish Agriculture in Early Historic Times', in *J.R.S.A.I.* LXXIV (1944).

Evans, E. E., and Gaffikin, M. 'Megaliths and Raths', in *Irish Naturalists' Journal*, V (1935).

Hencken, H. O'Neill. *Cahercommaun: A Stone Fort in Co. Clare*, Dublin, 1938.

Knox, H. T. 'Ruins of Cruachan A.1', in *J.R.S.A.I.* XLIV (1914).

Macalister, R. A. S., and Praeger, R. Ll. 'Report on the Excavation of Uisneach', in *P.R.I.A.* XXXVIII C (1928-9).

Ó Ríordáin, S. P. 'Excavations at Cush, Co. Limerick', in *P.R.I.A.* XLV C (1940).
and Foy, J. B. 'The Excavation of Leacanabuaile Stone Fort', in the *Journal of the Cork Historical and Archaeological Society*, XLVI (1941).

Proudfoot, V. B. 'The Economy of an Irish Rath', in *Medieval Archaeology*, V (1961).

Thomas, Charles. 'The Character and Origins of Roman Dumnonia', in *CBA Research Report 7*, London, 1966.

Westropp, T. J. 'The Ancient Forts of Ireland', in *T.R.I.A.* XXXI (1902).

CHAPTER 4

Collins, A. E. P., and Proudfoot, V. B. 'A Trial Escavation in Clea Lakes Crannóg, Co. Down', in *U.J.A.* XXII (1959).

Davies, Oliver. 'Excavations on the Dorsey and the Black Pig's Dykes', in *U.J.A.* III (1940).
'Contributions to the Study of Crannógs in Southern Ulster', in *U.J.A.* V (1942).
'Trial Excavation at Lough Enagh', in *U.J.A.* IV (1941).

de Vismes Kane, W. F. 'The Black Pig's Dyke: The Ancient Boundary Fortification of Uladh', in *P.R.I.A.* XXVII C (1908-9); and *P.R.I.A.* XXXIII C (1916-17).

Hayes-McCoy, G. A. (ed.). *Ulster and Other Irish Maps c. 1600*, Dublin, 1964.

Hughes, Kathleen. *The Church in Early Irish Society*, London, 1966.

Macalister, R. A. S. *Tara. A Pagan Sanctuary of Ancient Ireland*, London, 1931.

Ó Ríordáin, S. P. *Tara. The Monuments on the Hill*, Dundalk, 1954.

Westropp, T. J. 'Prehistoric Stone Forts of Northern Clare', in *J.R.S.A.I.* XXVII (1897).

Wood-Martin, W. G. *The Lake Dwellings of Ireland*, Dublin, 1886.

CHAPTER 5

Bigger, F. J. 'Inis Chlothrann (Inis Cleraun), Lough Ree: Its History and Antiquities', in *J.R.S.A.I.* XXX (1900).

Champheys, A. C. *Irish Ecclesiastical Architecture*, London, 1910.

Cochrane, R. 'Some notes on the Round Tower, etc., of Kilmacduagh', in *J.R.S.A.I.* XXXIV (1904).

Coffrey, G. *Guide to the Celtic Antiquities of the Christian Period*, Dublin, 1909.

Crawford, M. S. 'Ardpatrick, Co. Limerick', in *J.R.S.A.I.* XXXVIII (1908).

de Paor, Liam. 'A Survey of Sceilg Mhichíl', in *J.R.S.A.I.* LXXXV (1955).

Duignan, Michael. 'Early Monastic Site, Kiltiernan East Townland', in *J.R.S.A.I.* LXXXI (1951).

Fahey, J. 'Kilmacduagh and its Ecclesiastical Monuments', in *J.R.S.A.I.* XXXIV (1904).

ffrench, J. F. M. 'St. Mullins, Co. Carlow', in *J.R.S.A.I.* XXII (1892).

Kenny, J. F. *Sources for the Early History of Ireland: Ecclesiastical*, New York, 1929.

Lawlor, H. C. *The Monastery of St. Mochaoi of Nendrum*, Belfast, 1925.

BIBLIOGRAPHY

Lawlor, H. J. *Chapters on the Book of Mulling*, Edinburgh, 1897.

Leask, H. G. *Irish Churches and Monastic Buildings*, vol. I, Dundalk, 1955.
   Glendalough, (National Monuments Official Guide).

Lowry-Corry, Dorothy. 'St. Molaise's House at Devenish', in *J.R.S.A.I.* LXVI (1936).

Lucas, A. T. 'Irish-Norse Relations: Time for a Reappraisal', in *Journal of the Cork Historical and Archaeological Society*, LXXI 1966.
   'The Plundering and Burning of Churches in Ireland, 7th to 16th Century', in *North Munster Studies* 1967.

Macalister, R.A.S. 'The History and Antiquities of Inis Cealtra', in *P.R.I.A.* XXXIII C (1917).
   Monasterboice, Dundalk, 1946.

McKenna, J. E. *Devenish: Its History, Antiquities and Traditions*, Dublin (second edition), 1931.

Morris, Henry. 'Louthiana: Ancient and Modern', in the *Co. Louth Archaeological Journal*, I (1905) no. 2.

Ó Fiaích, An t-Athair Tómas. 'The Beginnings of Christianity', in *The Course of Irish History*, ed. by T. W. Moody and F. X. Martin, Cork, 1967.

Ryan, John. *Irish Monasticism, Origins and Early Development*, London, 1931.

Towill, E. S. 'Saint Mochaoi and Nendrum', in *U.J.A.* XXVII (1964).

Westropp, T. J. 'Notes on several Forts in Dunkellin and other parts of Southern Co. Galway', in *J.R.S.A.I.* XLIX (1919).

INDEX